Political Psychology

The World of Political Science—
The development of the discipline

Book series edited by
Michael Stein and John Trent

Professors **Michael B. Stein** and **John E. Trent** are the co-editors of the book series "The World of Political Science". The former is professor of Political Science at McMaster University in Hamilton, Ontario, Canada. The latter is a Fellow in the Center of Governance of the University of Ottawa, in Ottawa, Ontario, Canada, and a former professor in its Department of Political science.

Dr.**Tim Heinmiller** is the coordinator of the series, and Assistant Professor of Political Science at Brock University in St. Catherines, Ontario, Canada.

Linda Shepherd (ed.)

Political Psychology

Barbara Budrich Publishers
Opladen & Farmington Hills 2006

All rights reserved. No part of this publication may be reproduced, stored in or introduced into a retrieval system, or transmitted, in any form, or by any means (electronic, mechanical, photocopying, recording or otherwise) without the prior written permission of Barbara Budrich Publishers. Any person who does any unauthorized act in relation to this publication may be liable to criminal prosecution and civil claims for damages.

You must not circulate this book in any other binding or cover and you must impose this same condition on any acquirer.

A CIP catalogue record for this book is available from
Die Deutsche Bibliothek (The German Library)

© 2006 by Barbara Budrich Publishers, Opladen
www.barbara-budrich.net

ISBN 3-86649-027-5 (paperback)

Das Werk einschließlich aller seiner Teile ist urheberrechtlich geschützt. Jede Verwertung außerhalb der engen Grenzen des Urheberrechtsgesetzes ist ohne Zustimmung des Verlages unzulässig und strafbar. Das gilt insbesondere für Vervielfältigungen, Übersetzungen, Mikroverfilmungen und die Einspeicherung und Verarbeitung in elektronischen Systemen.

Die Deutsche Bibliothek – CIP-Einheitsaufnahme
Ein Titeldatensatz für die Publikation ist bei Der Deutschen Bibliothek erhältlich.

Verlag Barbara Budrich ⓑ Barbara Budrich Publishers
Stauffenbergstr. 7. D-51379 Leverkusen Opladen, Germany

28347 Ridgebrook. Farmington Hills, MI 48334. USA
www.barbara-budrich.net

Jacket illustration by disegno, Wuppertal, Germany – www.disenjo.de
Printed in Europe on acid-free paper by
Paper & Tinta, Poland

Contents

Foreword 9

Preface 11

1   Introduction: Research in Political Psychology at the
    Dawn of a New Century 13

2   The Infrastructure of Political Psychology 18
    2.1   Introduction 18
    2.2   Impact on the Discipline 20
    2.3   Education 23
    2.4   Resources 25
    2.5   Training Institutes, Workshops, and Seminars ... 27
    2.6   Books 29
    2.7   The Internet 31
    2.8   Research Funding 32
    2.9   Concluding Thoughts 34

3   Personality Theory in the Analysis of Political
    Leadership: Trends, Schemas, and Opportunities 36
    3.1   Early developments: Freud and the Repetition of Familial
          Adaptations 36
    3.2   Ego-psychology and Self Psychology: Political Applications   38
    3.3   Leader Personalities in the Context of Regime
          Characteristics 42
    3.4   Leadership style 47
    3.5   Developments for the Future: Leaders in Context ... 50
    3.5.1 Interrelations of Leaders 50
    3.5.2 Leaders and Advisers 53
    3.5.3 Leaders and Followers 54
    3.5.4 Differential Adaptations to Crises 56

5

3.5.5	Adaptation to the Environment	58
3.5.6	Conclusion	61

4 The Many Faces of International Political Psychology 63

4.1	Political Psychology as an Entity	65
4.2	Political Psychological Research in "Other" Countries	69
4.3	Theoretical Diversity	70
4.4	International Politics as the Focus of Research	71
4.5	Internationalization: The End Stage of a Process?	72
4.6	Lessons from (and for) Cultural Psychology	81
4.7	Conclusion	86
4.8	Author's Note	87

5 Political Psychology and the Study of Foreign Policy Decision Making ... 88

5.1	Introduction	88
5.2	Computational Approaches	89
5.2.1	Rule-Based Models	90
5.2.2	Belief Models	93
5.2.3	Hermeneutic Models	95
5.2.4	Computational Models: Final Thoughts	96
5.3	Experimental Approaches	98
5.3.1	Cognitive Structures	99
5.3.2	Cognitive Processes	100
5.4	Non-Experimental, Data Generation, and Observational Approaches	102
5.4.1	Pattern-Matching with Events Data	102
5.4.2	At-A-Distance Measures	103
5.5	Political Psychology and Social Constructivism	106
5.6	Conclusions: Do We Understand More About FPDM Through The Lens of Political Psychology?—and—Where Do We Go From Here?	106

6 Refocusing Political Psychology: The Search for a Twenty-First Century Agenda ... 110

- 6.1 The Real-World Foundations of Political Psychology ... 110
- 6.2 Globalization in the Twenty-First Century ... 111
- 6.2.1 Attractions and Preconditions of Globalization ... 113
- 6.2.2 Dangers and Risks of Globalization ... 114
- 6.2.3 Control, Legitimacy, and the Ironic Fate of Individualism .. 114
- 6.3 Threat and Paranoia ... 115
- 6.4 Inequality, Sense of Deserving, and Resentment ... 116
- 6.5 Skepticism and Malaise about Government ... 118
- 6.6 Charismatic Nationalism ... 120
- 6.7 Aggression ... 121
- 6.8 Response of the Globalizers ... 121
- 6.9 The Agenda for Political Psychology ... 121
- 6.10 How Do We Get To This New Agenda? ... 122
- 6.10.1 What Psychology Can Provide ... 122
- 6.10.2 What Political Science Can Provide ... 123
- 6.10.3 Statistics ... 123
- 6.10.4 Beyond Psychology and Political Science ... 124
- 6.10.5 A Plea for Methodological Pluralism ... 125
- 6.11 Conclusion ... 127

7 Concluding Remarks: Developments and Trends in Political Psychology ... 128

- 7.1 Overview ... 128
- 7.2 Interdisciplinary Successes and Challenges ... 128

References ... 135

About the Editor and Contributors ... 156

Index ... 160

This volume is dedicated to all those
who embark upon interdisciplinary research

Foreword

This volume of the "World of Political Science" series, initiated by the International Political Science Association (IPSA) and Research Committee 33, evaluates the development of the transdiscipline of political Psychology, a sub-field of both political science and psychology. Each volume of the series is being prepared by leading international scholars representing one of the research committees of IPSA. There may be as many as 20 volumes in the series over the next three years.

"The World of Political Science" series is intended to fulfill several objectives. First, it aims to provide an up-to-date, analytical overview of the various sub-fields of political science. Second, although prepared by leading academic specialists, the Series is intended to be accessible both to students of the field and those who want to learn more about it. Third, in addition to the state-of-the-art overview, the books seek to offer an explanation of how the field has evolved into what it is today. Thus, it serves as part of a broader objective of evaluating the current state of development of political science. Fourth, on the basis of this evaluation, the volume editors and authors make proposals for the improvement of each sub-field and eventually, for the discipline as a whole. Fifth, coming from the Research Committees of an international association, the Series desires to be as international and comparative as possible, but this may vary according to the subject matter of each volume.

It is entirely appropriate that the second volume in the Series should be devoted to the subject of political psychology. Because of the manner in which the discipline of political science is taught, it is not often recognized that interdisciplinary research is one of the predominant ways of studying politics. For example, in the International Political Science Association there are interdisciplinary Research Committees that focus on religion, ethnicity, geography, biology, gender, communications, and politics as well as on political sociology and political economy. Because of both its scope and applicability, interdisciplinary research can search for and discover broad patterns of development.

This can be seen in the varying definitions of political psychology, which Kathleen McGraw in this volume has characterized as "concerned with the causes, dynamics, and consequences of human thinking and action in the context of politics. It is concerned with causal processes working in two directions: the impact of psychological processes on the unfolding of political behaviour as well as the impact of political events on psychological processes." In practical terms this means, as Peter Suedfeld and Ian Hansen have pointed out, "there is lively theorizing and research about war and peace, political and social identity, socialization, intergroup relations (including those related to ethnicity, gender and socio-economic class), political ideologies and attitudes, democracy and human rights, conflict resolution, voting patterns and political leadership." Some of us have intuitive predispositions toward psychological behaviour. Others prefer to raise large questions within this perspective. Either type of reader will find the accumulated knowledge in this book both instructive and fascinating.

We want to express our profound appreciation to the editor of the volume, Linda Shepherd, for her initiative and persistence in this publication, and to the authors and members of Research Committee 29 on Political Psychology for their notable contributions to it. We also acknowledge our deep gratitude to the Social Science and Humanities Research Council of Canada (SSHRC), whose initial Research Development Initiatives Grant #820-1999-1022 and later extensions made the project possible. We are also grateful to the Executive Committee of the International Political Science Association for its initial encouragement of the project by permitting us to establish special panels on sub-disciplinary development at the 2000 Quebec IPSA World Congress, and for its pledge to fund the copyediting and indexing of later volumes in the series through its Committee on Research and Training. For their contributions to this endeavour, we gratefully acknowledge the work of the Project Sub-Committee of IPSA Research Committee 33 on the Study of Political Science as a Discipline whose members include: Henrik Bang, David Easton, James Farr, John Gunnell, Takashi Inoguchi, Adele Jinada, and Klaus von Beyme. Finally, a special word of thanks is owed to our Project Coordinator, Tim Heinmiller, who applied his considerable academic and administrative capabilities to all major concerns of this Series.

Of course, ultimate responsibility for the series belongs to us, the co-editors. This project has been a joint and equal collaborative effort on our part right from its beginning, and we are very pleased to see this effort come to fruition.

Michael Stein (McMaster University)
John Trent (University of Ottawa)

Preface

This volume of the "World of Political Science" series, initiated by the International Political Science Association (IPSA) and Research Committee 33, evaluates the development of the transdiscipline of political psychology, a sub-field of both political science and psychology. Research Committee 29 of the International Political Science Association, devoted to the study of political psychology, embarked upon this valuable enterprise and presents this book to provide information about the developing infrastructure of political psychology, the evolution of concepts and theories within political psychology, international developments in the field, current concepts and methodology, and trends which augur for the future of the enterprise. This volume includes several critical evaluations of the state of research in political psychology. It also provides suggestions for continued research in this new era. Research that will, in an increasingly globalized context; make significant contributions through theoretical, methodological, and conceptual breakthroughs at the intersection of political science and psychology.

It has been a pleasure to work with the contributors to this volume, each chosen because of their significant contributions to the field of political psychology and their present and past leadership roles in international organizations devoted to the development of the discipline. I would like to extend my appreciation to each of them for their considerable efforts and for chapters that establish a foundation for the next generation of research in the field.

A debt of gratitude is also owed to the series editors John Trent and Michael Stein, their assistant Tim Heinmiller, and three anonymous reviewers. I would like to express my thanks to the Chair of Research Committee 29, Ofer Feldman, for energetic leadership of the committee and thoughtful consultation. Finally an important note of gratitude to my husband Andrew and my children for their cheerful and constant support throughout each and every research project.

Linda Shepherd (Cal Poly)
San Luis Obispo, California

1 Introduction: Research in Political Psychology at the Dawn of a New Century

Linda Shepherd

Political psychology exists as an interdisciplinary subfield of two well-established disciplines; from this position it naturally came to encompass a wide range of components, all uniquely equipped to investigate the intersection of human psychology and political phenomena. Scholars who specialize in political psychology have generated considerable momentum, developing their own journal, creating an international society that sponsors yearly conferences, providing for specialized training in the field, and stimulating a great deal of relevant research. This volume establishes the state of research in political psychology as well as the state of infrastructure in the subfield during this, the first decade of the new century. As political psychology is characterized by research which benefits from both of the parent disciplines; chapters in this volume have come from those who specialize in political science as well as those whose department of origin is psychology.

The fertile foundation of interdisciplinary scholarship in political psychology has resulted in research that continually evolves, evaluating events, issues, and individuals with a lens that supports diverse theoretical applications. These applications range from public opinion to elite decision-making; from intergroup conflict to political leadership; from theories of personality development, individual cognition, and individual motivation to mass political behavior, international conflict, and mass communication. As these topics imply, analyses in political psychology evaluate the collective as well as the individual, with concerns that are multiple and embrace personality, behavior, cognition, process, and context, as well as interactions between any or all of these. Political psychology seeks to enhance understanding of the myriad of precursors leading to individual and collective behavior.

It has been argued that any successful interdisciplinary field is preceded, indeed, foreshadowed, by a need to solve practical problems (cf. Klein, 1996; Messer-Davidow, Shumway, & Sylvan, 1993). For political psychology, the advent and events of World War II served as important stimuli for interdisciplinary scholarship that proceeded to evaluate the role of personality in leader and follower behavior, the use of psychological warfare, political socialization, and the development of personality as it is related to decision making, cognition, and motivation within the individual psyche.

The opportunity to bring psychological and political theories to bear in explaining political phenomena has been made even more powerful by the use of multiple methodologies drawn from each discipline and capable of use in crosscultural contexts. Whether quantitative or qualitative, experimental or survey, content analytic or psychodiagnostic; methodological approaches in political psychology benefit from the willingness of scholars to blend and apply relevant and diverse techniques to effectively assess personality, orientation, and behavior. As the chapters in this volume indicate, unique methods have and will continue to be developed to allow and enhance the measurement of key variables relevant to theories within the corpus of political psychology.

While this book is in large part a response to the International Political Science Association's vision of a series of handbooks that would establish a baseline for future development and research in each of the subfields of political science, it also offers a significant contribution to the field of political psychology. The chapters contained herein describe, evaluate, and track the development of the subfield of political psychology, in infrastructure as well as theory. The authors provide important explanations for the evolution and current state of political psychology, they identify major developments that affect and define the specialization, discuss factors accounting for these developments, investigate the major approaches to the subfield, deal with the practical application of research in political psychology, discuss trends, and evaluate current resources. The volume begins with an evaluation of the state of infrastructure in political psychology.

Kathleen McGraw orients her evaluation of infrastructure with a discussion of the theoretical placement of political psychology within the two disciplines from which it grew, with observations regarding the influence of political psychology in each of its parent fields. Her detailed investigation of infrastructure in the subfield includes analyses of national and international resources in the area of education, professional associations, and research. She also provides evidence of the increasing presence of political psychology in the major journals of political science and reports on the current parameters of undergraduate and graduate coursework and programs in political psychology. McGraw provides important information about the ongoing development of NSF funding for research relevant to agendas within political psychology and describes developed programs within private foundations that have the potential of expanding opportunities for funding and training in political psychology. McGraw also provides commentary on current research with specific discussion of public policy implications and the possibility of synthesis between "positive political (rational choice) theory and behavioral approaches to judgment and decision making."

In their chapter "Personality Theory in the Analysis of Political Leadership: Trends, Schemas, and Opportunities," Elizabeth Marvick and Betty Glad discuss and analyze the development of political psychology as influenced by theories of personality. Personality theories are traced as they emerged from early origins to become integral components in the analysis of political leadership. The authors provide several detailed examples from psychoanalytic studies of political leaders, demonstrating the application of a variety of analytic techniques, including depth psychology, ego psychology, and narcissistic processes to understanding linkages between personality and political behavior. Illustrations include Abraham Lincoln, Woodrow Wilson, Winston Churchill, George Washington, Mohandas Gandhi, Nelson Mandela, Mustafa Kemal, Dwight D. Eisenhower, and Charles de Gaulle, among others. The authors investigate findings that clarify connections between individual personality, goal definition, relationships, and adaptation to the political environment. Relationships between leaders and advisors receive particular attention with discussion of operative psychic mechanisms that serve to enhance affective ties and thereby increase the influence of advisors, some of whom emerge as strategic actors. Marvick and Glad also evaluate the application of personality theory to relationships between leaders and followers, discussing psychological processes which underlie follower propensities to view, idealize, and mirror their leaders. Throughout the chapter, the authors carefully evaluate the role of personality *and* institutional environments as significant influences of political behavior and perception.

The development of political psychology as an international enterprise is evaluated by Peter Suedfeld and Ian Hansen in their chapter "The Many Faces of International Political Psychology." Suedfeld and Hansen provide a detailed discussion of the international scope of the discipline including overviews of international theoretical developments, international theoretical diversity, international collaboration, and publications with specific international focus. Adair's empirical markers of internationalization are adapted and employed to synthesize an investigation of the degree to which the discipline of political psychology has been internationalized. The authors expand upon the Adair stages, identifying two additional stages relevant to the process of internationalization experienced within the subfield of political psychology particularly, and the social sciences generally. The predominance of western models (North American and European) is considered with commentary on the roles played by recognized norms of scientific research and the standard publication process. The authors direct readers to consider the internationalization of cultural psychology, pointing out that lessons learned in this subfield would benefit political psychology, providing "rich sources of hypotheses and guiding theories for international political psychology." Incorporation of concepts and theories that are fully cognizant of cultural influences and cultural constraints is critical to the formation of robust theory in a fully internationalized political psychology. Suedfeld and Hansen find that political psychology has grown as an international enterprise and encourage continued interaction and feedback between non-Western cultural traditions and the substance and theory of political psychology.

Donald Sylvan and Brent Strathman's article "Political Psychology and the Study of Foreign Policy Decision Making" provides a discussion of applied political psychology from within the domain of international relations and foreign policy decision making (FPDM). Sylvan and Strathman demonstrate the ways in which scholarly research in FPDM has benefited from an interdisciplinary approach to research and from the many attributes of those trained in political psychology. They evaluate the manner by which research in applied computer systems, designed to simulate the processes and structure of decision making, fits within the corpus of political psychology literature. The authors provide insights into information processing and foreign policy decision making while reviewing relevant research from both disciplines.

David Winter's article "Refocusing Political Psychology: The Search for a Twenty-First Century Agenda" examines the origins of political psychology, discusses current challenges in the subfield, and offers specific recommendations for a dynamic and influential future. His essay provides a rich historical resource for the reader interested in early influences on the subfield. In so doing, he presents an analytical overview of political psychology as an interdisciplinary response to critical events within the twentieth century. Political psychology is presented as a lens from which to analyze individuals, events, and trends, and as a natural progression from efforts to understand the psychological foundations of the democratic process, leadership, and inter-state relations. Winter's evaluation of the current state of research in political psychology proceeds from within the context of increased and ubiquitous globalization. He reviews intellectual, methodological, and educational agendas that will be influenced by escalating bureaucracies of globalization transcending national and cultural boundaries and resulting in transformations in perception, behavior, and political response. Winter draws from a wide variety of literary, political, and psychological resources to evaluate the attributes of a political psychology operating at the crossroads of technological, economic, corporate, and media globalization. He argues that political psychology is uniquely positioned to provide insightful analysis of the psychological and political effects of twenty-first century changes. The evolution of modern industrial capitalism is affecting individual perception, psychology, and behavior, and it is influencing governance, legitimacy, and bureaucratic conduct. Issues of income inequality, political and psychological responses to relative deprivation, ethnic stratification, nationalism, prejudice, and violence, each inform this final chapter's analysis of the evolution of political psychology. The intricate political and psychological issues of skepticism, cynicism, and corruption, as well as the erosion of political and economic institutions are encompassed by the sweeping scope of Winter's treatment. Concluding that the forces of globalization are not only changing political and economic interactions but also affecting the work of political psychology, Winter evaluates the roles of psychology, political science, statistics, and history, in sustaining and enriching research agendas within the political psychology of the twenty-first century.

2 The Infrastructure of Political Psychology

Kathleen M. McGraw

2.1 Introduction

Everyone that possesses a nodding scholarly acquaintance with the phrase *political psychology* understands that it is the intellectual activity that takes place at the intersection of political science and psychology. Beyond the broad consensual acceptance of this Venn diagrammatic designation, a variety of definitions and conceptualizations have been put forth (see the contributions in Monroe 2002, for thoughtful discussions). These various definitions are characterized not so much by disagreements about core principles but rather differences in emphasis. I suspect most political psychologists are comfortable with a conceptualization of political psychology as the scholarly activity concerned with understanding the causes, dynamics, and consequences of human thinking and action in the context of politics. It is concerned with causal processes working in two directions: the impact of psychological processes on the unfolding of political behavior as well as the impact of political events on psychological processes.

Because political psychology is an inherently interdisciplinary exercise, it is possible to examine it from at the lens of each parent discipline, psychology and political science. However, the task before me in this chapter is to describe the infrastructure of political psychology as it pertains to the discipline of political science. As a consequence, I have little to say about the status of political psychology in the discipline of psychology. It certainly would be a very different portrait than the one that is developed in this chapter, as most indicators suggest that political psychology has been more valued within, and has had more of an impact upon, political science than on psychology (see Krosnick 2002, and Krosnick and McGraw 2002, for discussions).[1]

---

[1] There are some indications suggesting that political psychology is achieving an increased legitimacy and presence within psychology, and in particular, within social psychology. For example, there has been an increase in the number of graduate students from social psychology participating in the OSU Summer Institute in Political Psychology in recent years. Political scientists have published political psychology essays in the *Annual Review of Psychology* series (eg, Sullivan and Transue 1999, Iyengar and Simon 2000, and Graber 2004). Also, the most recent edition of the prestigious *Handbook of Social Psychology* contains two chapters explicitly devoted to political psychology (Kinder 1998, and Tetlock 1998).

Because my focus is on political science, I adopt a view of political psychology that is close to that articulated by Peg Hermann, namely that of political psychology as a *perspective* that can be useful for "understanding politics no matter the issue, topic or problem under consideration" (2002: 46). There are other perspectives in political science, most prominently, political economy, from which political science also borrows, and which is often viewed by political psychologists as the opponent in the struggle for the soul of political science (Jervis 1989, Sears 1989). Treating political psychology as a perspective has two broad concrete ramifications. First, in her analysis (and I concur), Hermann rejects a view of political psychology as a *field* or *discipline*, in the sense of having a circumscribed subject matter, set of conceptual parameters, and methodological techniques. Rather, political psychology is fully contained within the parent disciplines of political science and psychology. There are no "Departments of Political Psychology," at least in the United States, and there are no scholars, with the possible exception of a handful who may hold named chairs, who are designated "Professor of Political Psychology." That said, political psychology does have many of the accouterments of a disciplinary field, such as scholarly associations, journals, and meetings. I will make use of the language of "field" or "discipline" when talking about political psychology, because that is common in our discourse, but with the understanding that this term is used in a more limited sense than when we talk about the fields of political science or psychology.

Second, treating political psychology as a perspective within political science signals a lack of boundaries in terms of substantive topics, as well as an endorsement of methodological pluralism. As a consequence, political psychologists can and do apply the psychological perspective to a wide-range of political phenomena. As Bar-Tal (2002) has documented, cognitive social psychological theory has had the greatest impact on political psychology scholarship, although other grand theoretical frameworks also have a presence. Likewise, political psychologists can and do make use of a variety of methodological tools, including experiments, surveys, case studies, focus groups, elite interviews, and content and discourse analysis. Even with theoretical and methodological diversity, unifying parameters can be identified. First, political psychology is ultimately focused on the individual as the unit of analysis. This does not preclude understanding the impact of collectives on the individual, nor with understanding how individual actors within collectives aggregate to produce collective outcomes. Second, political psychologists are concerned with process, that is, with understanding the causal dynamics that produce the phenomena under study. Third, political psychology recognizes the power of the situation and context-specific factors in shaping political behaviors and decisions. Lewin's (1936) classic formulation, "Behavior = f(Person, Environment)," provides an explanatory framework that pushes us to develop ever-stronger theoretical statements about the "conditions under which" political outcomes are more or less likely to occur (see Smith 1968, McGuire 1969, 1983, Sniderman, Brody, and Tetlock 1991, and Herrmann, Tetlock, and Visser 1999, for prominent political psychological examples making use of the Lewinian framework).

Having laid out, in broad strokes, the parameters of political psychology, the goal of the remainder of this chapter is to take stock of the current infrastructure and resources available to political psychologists, as well as to other scholars interested in learning more about the political psychological perspective. There are four sections. First, to motivate the undertaking, I provide evidence about the increasing impact of political psychology on the discipline of political science. I then describe the educational programs that serve as the lifeblood of the field. Third, I describe a variety of resources in political psychology, including professional associations, books, training institutes, the Internet, and research funding. Finally, I end with some concluding comments. The chapter has a decided focus on the United States, because, at least at the time of this writing, most of the elements of the infrastructure of political psychology are centered in the United States.[2]

2.2 Impact on the Discipline

At the start of the new millennium, political psychology would seem to be at a propitious position, in terms of its status and legitimacy within the discipline of political science. This is not to say that interdisciplinary scholarship is easy to engage in successfully or that political psychology enjoys a dominant position within the discipline. Certainly, some subfields in political psychology—such as public opinion and some areas of international politics—are better accepted by the mainstream of political science than others (Jervis 1989). Some commentators might recall earlier "glory days"; for example, David Sears claimed that "the early 1960s were the palmy days of psychology's influence in political science" (1989: 501). Ultimately, we should move beyond subjective impressions to more objective indicators to gauge the impact of political psychology on the discipline.

---

2   For discussions of the state of political psychology outside the United States see Ardila (Latin America, 1996); Bryder (Western Europe, 1986); Feldman (Japan, 1990); Lamare and Milburn (New Zealand, 1990); Montero (Latin America, 1986); Montiel and Chiongbian (Philippines, 1991); Pye (Asia, 1986); Shumao (China, 1996).

One indicator of impact, and one that is amenable to systematic analysis, is references in scholarly journals. I searched the political science journals archived in JSTOR[3] for variations on the phrase "political psychology" to examine temporal trends. Note that this is not an analysis of journal articles that are *about* topics that are analyzed from a political psychological perspective, a more difficult and time consuming enterprise that would also no doubt be more interesting as it would shed light on questions about the success rate of political psychological research in general, and specific topics in particular.[4] It is clear that this analysis is simultaneously too conservative and too liberal. It is conservative in the sense that key political psychological articles are missed. For example, Greenstein's classic article, the "Benevolent Leader" (1960), is not counted as it does not include the relevant phrases. It is also a fairly liberal criterion of impact, as any mention of the phrase, no matter how limited or tangential to the topic at hand, is counted. Moreover, readers should be aware that base number of journals is not constant, as scholarly journal outlets, in political science as in all disciplines, increased throughout the 20th century. Finally, because the journal *Political Psychology* is not archived as a political science journal in JSTOR, the numbers do not include those publications, but do include citations of *Political Psychology* articles in other journals.

Despite all of these limitations, this temporal analysis should prove informative as one indicator of the evolving presence and vitality of political psychology in the discipline of political science. Table 1 summarizes the results from the JSTOR search by decade, starting with the 1920s and going through the end of the 1990s. The first column provides the frequencies of mentions of "political psychology" and its variants in all of the political science journals archived in JSTOR, whereas the second column is limited to the three widely regarded as the most influential generalist journals: *American Political Science Review, American Journal of Political Science,* and *Journal of Politics* (Giles, Mizell, and Patterson 1989). The pattern is quite clear: references to "political psychology" increased throughout the decades of the 20th century, and in particular showed sizable jumps from the 1970s on. The same pattern is evident in the analysis limited to the "big 3" political science journals, suggesting that

---

3 JSTOR is an electronic archive of back issues of scholarly journals, generally available through institutional subscription.
4 Rahn, Sullivan and Rudolph (2002) analyzed the content of the *APSR, AJPS,* and *JOP* during the 1980s and 1990s. Articles utilizing a political psychological perspective averaged about 20% of the total published, with no increase during those two decades. However, they did find an increase in the prominence of articles reflecting a rational choice perspective over this time period, particularly in the flagship journal of the discipline, the *APSR*

political psychology's increased presence occurred in the mainstream of the discipline, and so was not limited to more secondary topics and publication outlets.

Table 2-1: References to "Political Psychology" in Scholarly Journals

Decade	Political Science	Political Science ("Big 3") [a]	Sociology	Economics
1920s	17	14	8	3
1930s	14	6	4	7
1940s	35	12	11	15
1950s	38	9	7	12
1960s	53	10	10	19
1970s	109	30	30	12
1980s	159	48	32	3
1990s	262	106	57	3

Note: The entries are the number of references to "political psychology" and its variants in each decade in the disciplinary scholarly journals archived in JSTOR.

a   *American Political Science Review, American Journal of Political Science,* and *Journal of Politics.*

For purposes of comparison, I also searched for "political psychology" and its variants in the sociology and economics journals archived in JSTOR.[5] Those results are summarized in the last two columns of Table 1. Although commentators have long included sociology as one of the disciplines with a close alliance to political psychology, references in sociology journals historically have been, and continue to be, relatively sparse.[6] Finally, probably to no one's surprise, political psychology does not have much of a presence in scholarly economics journals, and if anything, that presence decreased in the latter part of the 20th century rather than increased.

In short, the trends displayed in Table 1 suggest a reasonably optimistic portrait of the increasing vitality and impact of political psychology on the discipline of political science. But lest political psychologists become overly

---

5   Although a similar examination of psychology journals would obviously be desirable, psychology journals are not archived in JSTOR, nor are they available in any other full-text electronic archive, so that analysis is impossible.

6   There is some overlap in the sociology and political science journal numbers, as two journals *(Public Opinion Quarterly* and *Journal of Palestinian Studies)* are present in both disciplinary archives.

complacent, one more analysis suggests a more sobering account. I did a parallel search of the political science journals for the phrase "political economy" and its variants, in order to compare the presence of that other prominent perspective in political science. Those numbers are so large as to dwarf completely the numbers found for "political psychology" references. Whereas the frequencies for "political psychology" and its variants were 109, 159, and 262 in the 1970s, 1980s, and 1990s, respectively, the frequencies for "political economy" and its variants are greater by several magnitudes (specifically, 818, 2071, and 2111, in the same three decades). In other words, a random individual engaging in a random perusal of a random political science journal published in the 1990s was eight times more likely to encounter a reference to "political economy" than "political psychology." Jervis (1989) and Sears (1989) have fretted about the greater influence of economics than psychology on the discipline of political science, and these numbers can be taken as one illustration of the magnitude of that differential influence.

2.3 Education

In order for any scholarly perspective to survive, it must reproduce itself, producing new scholars who both internalize and challenge the conventional wisdom. Formal educational programs for the training of political psychologists are a relatively recent development. The first graduate program in political psychology was founded at Yale University in 1969. The Yale program was unique because it led to a double PhD in political science and psychology, and so it required a full course load in both disciplines. Currently, to the best of my knowledge, formal doctoral programs in political psychology exist at SUNY-Stony Brook (founded in 1979), University of Wisconsin (1982), CUNY-Graduate Center (1988), UC-Irvine (1989), UCLA (1989), the Ohio State University (1990), George Washington University (1992), University of Minnesota (1995), and Washington State University (1996). Sadly, the Yale program ceased to exist in the 1990s. These doctoral programs vary on a number of dimensions: whether political psychology is a major or minor field of study (in most programs, it is a minor); whether the program is housed in one department (usually Political Science) or is more fully interdisciplinary; and in the breadth of the course offerings and faculty specializations. Contrary to the founding Yale model, none of the current programs require full training in both psychology and political science.

Because political psychology is increasingly viewed as a legitimate and valuable perspective in political science, a number of programs in the United States have a "critical mass" of faculty interested in political psychology and those programs allow students to create individualized courses of study that have a strong emphasis in political psychology (as opposed to a formal concentration; these programs include Michigan, North Carolina, Duke, Berkeley, Princeton, Rutgers, Columbia, Syracuse, and the University of Chicago). Finally, there are few formal programs outside of the United States; Dana Ward reports that degree-granting programs in political psychology exist at the University of Melbourne, Berlin Free University, Copenhagen, Hebrew University, and the London School of Economics (2002, see Sears and Funk 1991, and Ward 2002, for more detailed discussions of graduate training in political psychology).

Although the number of formal programs in political psychology is limited, graduate coursework in political psychology is fairly common. Sears and Funk (1991) conducted a survey to assess the prevalence of political psychology in graduate education. They concluded that most major American universities offer some graduate coursework in political psychology, that those courses are more often offered in political science rather than psychology departments, and that those courses tend to focus on subsets of the field rather than provide omnibus overviews of the field as a whole. I doubt that much has changed in the political psychology graduate landscape since Sears and Funk's survey, and if anything, would estimate that graduate courses reflecting a political psychological perspective have increased. I say this because some "mainstream" political science topics, such as public opinion and foreign policy analysis, are impossible to teach properly without incorporating a solid dose of political psychology because contemporary advances in those substantive topics have been so strongly influenced by psychological theories and methods.

Unlike exposure to the parent disciplines of political science or psychology, it is more often than not the case that students first encounter political psychology at the graduate level, rather than in their undergraduate curriculum. I suspect most academics who are actively engaged in teaching and research in political psychology have had encounters with students along the lines of "I wish I had known political psychology existed!" earlier in their education. Although political psychology courses are taught at the undergraduate level, most commonly in the universities that have graduate programs and a critical mass of faculty, we have little systematic data on the current prevalence and nature of the undergraduate political psychology experience (Funk and Sears 1991, provide some data about undergraduate courses in the late 1980s). I do not know of any college or university that has an undergraduate major in political psychology, although the possibility of such a major is apparently under discussion at the Claremont Colleges (Levin 2000; see this article more generally for a useful discussion of the challenges and rewards of teaching political psychology to undergraduates, as well as resources and suggestions about the content and structure of such courses). More than a decade ago, David Sears made a heartfelt call for political psychologists to engage in more proselytizing for the discipline, and that as part of this process "we need to make sure that political psychology is taught to undergraduates, and to large numbers of them" (1989: 506). This call is as important in the 21st century—if political psychology is to sustain itself and flourish, more students will need to be introduced to the field earlier in the educational process.

2.4 Resources

Professional Associations

The primary professional association for political psychologists is the International Society of Political Psychology (ISPP, at http://ispp.org). ISPP was established in 1978, with Jeanne Knutson serving as the founder and first Executive Director. As the name suggests, ISPP has always been explicitly *international* in scope, rather than modeled on national scholarly associations such as the American Political Science Association or American Psychological Association. ISPP has approximately 1330 members (as of June 2002); about two-thirds (875) of the membership is from the United States. Other countries with at least a double-digit membership presence in ISPP are Australia (17), Canada (35), Germany (34), Israel (40), Italy (15), Japan (26), Mexico (13), Netherlands (36), Spain (20), and the United Kingdom (32). Most of the ISPP membership lists either political science (590) or psychology (506) as their disciplinary affiliation.[7] Outside of the two parent disciplines, ISPP has members from a wide array of academic disciplines, reflecting its interdisciplinary focus (the two most common affiliations, after political science and psychology, are sociology and psychiatry, with 61 and 55 members, respectively).

ISPP is active on a number of fronts in promoting and cultivating political psychology. It publishes the eponymous journal *Political Psychology,* which steadily moved up in citation rankings during the 1990s. According to the Journal Citation Reports published by the Institute for Scientific Information (ISI) for the year 2000, *Political Psychology* ranked

---

7 Thanks to Heather Gillespie for providing these membership data.

13th out of top journals in Political Science (up from its ranking of 27th in 1999) and 19th out of top Social Psychology journals (up from its ranking of 27th in 1999; these data are reported at http://ispp.org/announcements/ JulyReport2002. htm).

ISPP also publishes a newsletter *ISPPNews* (back issues are available at the ISPP homepage), and is beginning an annual book series, *Advances in Political Psychology,* edited by Margaret Hermann. It has also committed to continuing publication of new editions of the *Handbook of Political Psychology* at ten-year intervals; the most recent volume edited by David Sears, Leonie Huddy, and Bob Jervis was published in 2003. The association sponsors an annual conference that meets on a cyclical basis in various locations in the world. It confers awards annually for distinguished contributions to the discipline (specifically, the Lasswell Award for Distinguished Scientific Contributions, the Sanford Award for Distinguished Professional Contributions, and the Erikson Award for Early Career Achievement). It has a very active and collegial Junior Scholars Committee. The ISPP homepage contains a wealth of information about political psychology degree programs, course information (including a syllabi collection), and links to a large variety of on-line resources relevant to political psychology.

The American Political Science Association (APSA, at http://apsanet. org) has approximately 13,500 members. There is an organized section for Political Psychology (Section 28), which has about 400 dues-paying members.[8] The section organizes panels for the Annual Meeting, since 1994 has conferred the Robert E. Lane Best Book Award for the best book on political psychology published in the previous year, and it publishes a newsletter, *The Political Psychologist,* currently edited by Chuck Taber, Stanley Feldman, and Leonie Huddy at SUNY—Stony Brook (back issues of the newsletter are available online at http:// www. sunysb. edu/pol sci).

The International Political Science Association (IPSA, online at http:// www.ipsa-aisp.org) has about 1000 individual members, and is made up of 51 Research Committees, including the Psycho-Politics Research Committee (RC 29), which is responsible for the publication of this volume. RC 29 sponsors panels at international conferences, and it publishes a newsletter that details the research and other activities of its members (RC 29 newsletters are archived at http://www.ipsa-psychopolitics.nl).

---

8 Although this figure is small as an overall percentage of the total APSA membership, it should be noted that membership in an organized section of APSA requires additional dues, so the number of members who join any organized sections is relatively low. Only one of the 36 organized sections has more than 1000 members.

The International Studies Association (ISA, online at http://www.isanet.org) has about 3,000 members. Although it does not have a section explicitly devoted to Political Psychology, its sections on Foreign Policy Analysis, Peace Studies, and Ethnicity include a number of political psychologists, and the websites for those sections contain various resources (syllabi, newsletters) that should be of interest to many political psychologists.

2.5 Training Institutes, Workshops, and Seminars

Although graduate courses and programs of study exist, it is nonetheless the case that many students and professionals interested in political psychology do not have access to training in the field. Even students in formal political psychology programs typically do not receive a broad training in political psychological theory and methodology. The Summer Institute in Political Psychology at Ohio State University was established to provide broad and extensive training in political psychology. The idea of establishing a summer training institute in political psychology was developed as part of a 1988 ISPP 10-year plan for the society's future. The first SIPP was held in 1991, and it occurred annually every summer up through 2003 at Ohio State (for more details about the history of SIPP, see Krosnick and Hermann 1993, Wituski, Clawson, Oxley, Green and Barr 1998). Sponsored by ISPP, financial support for SIPP has been provided by various units at Ohio State, in particular the Mershon Center, the Departments of Political Science and Psychology, the College of Social and Behavioral Sciences, and the Office of Continuing Education. Directorship of SIPP has been shared by various Ohio State faculty members, including Margaret Hermann and Jon Krosnick (the founding directors), as well as Marilynn Brewer, Rick Herrmann, Kathleen McGraw, Tom Nelson, Wendy Rahn, and Phil Tetlock. For a variety of reasons, Ohio State decided to discontinue its sponsorship of SIPP in 2003. Happily for the field, Stanford University has stepped in to revive SIPP in 2005 (directed again by Jon Krosnick; see http://www.stanford.edu/group/sipp).

SIPP is a three- to four-week long workshop for junior scholars (advanced graduate students and junior faculty) and policy analysts who are interested in receiving advanced training in the concepts and methods of political psychology. SIPP is structured to accomplish three goals (Krosnick and Hermann 1993): academic (to provide broad exposure to relevant scholarly work in political science and psychology); professional development (how to succeed in an interdisciplinary career); and institution building (to create a network of political psychologists). The curriculum and focus of SIPP has evolved over its 15 year existence. In its earliest years, the SIPP curriculum was divided into psychology and political science lectures, with the integration of those topics achieved in the context of small discussion groups. As the field of political psychology matured, the curriculum has gradually evolved to focus more explicitly on political psychological topics. Although in its broad parameters the SIPP curriculum has been relatively stable, it is not invariant, in order to be able to accommodate the increasingly large number of political psychology scholars and topics as well as to be able to introduce new developments in political psychology scholarship.

Enrollment in SIPP has been remarkably steady over the course of its existence, averaging about 50 participants each summer, so that more than 600 individuals have completed the training program as of 2003. These include students and faculty from universities around the world, as well as professionals in policy making positions from a variety of governmental organizations (United States and international). Perhaps the major accomplishment of SIPP has been to create a network of junior scholars who are committed to political psychology and who as a result of that commitment sustain and bolster ISPP and the discipline.

Because interest in political psychology is worldwide, and because the costs of attending the Ohio-based SIPP can be prohibitive for international students, there has been a longstanding interest in establishing a parallel summer training institute outside of the United States. The summer of 2002 marked the inaugural session of the European Summer Institute in Political Psychology in Warsaw (ESIPP, at http://www.swps.edu.pl/esipp). Sponsored by ISPP and organized by the Warsaw School of Social Psychology in Poland, ESIPP is a two-week training program focusing on core theoretical and methodological issues in political psychology, with a special focus on issues relevant to European countries. The founding directors of ESIPP are Janusz Reykowski and Daniel Bar-Tal. As of this writing, the future of ESIPP was uncertain, and interested readers should consult the ESIPP homepage for information about future sessions.

The Solomon Asch Center at the University of Pennsylvania (at http://www.psych.upenn.edu/sacsec) sponsors a Summer Institute on ethnopolitical conflict and its mental health consequences. Begun in 1999, the Institute is offered during alternative years, and consists of a ten-week program that is broadly interdisciplinary. Selected Fellows from the Summer Institute receive support for follow-up research and clinical work at international sites of ethnic conflict, such as in Northern Ireland, Israel/Palestine, and South Africa.

In addition to these summer institutes, a number of universities offer regular workshops and seminars in political psychology that provide scholars the opportunity to present their research to interested audiences. Four are noteworthy. First, since 1989, political psychologists in the vicinity of New

York City have met biannually for a full-day seminar at Columbia University. The Columbia Seminar on Political Psychology, with support from the Paul F. Lazarsfeld Center for the Social Sciences at Columbia's Institute for Social and Economic Research and Policy, is organized by Bob Shapiro, Leonie Huddy, and Stanley Feldman. Second, Harvard's biweekly Political Psychology and Behavior Workshop, begun in the Fall of 2000, provides an interdisciplinary forum for the presentation and discussion of current research that uses a psychological and empirical orientation to examine the microfoundations of citizen and elite behavior. The Harvard Workshop is supported by the Center for Basic Research in the Social Sciences, directed by Jim Alt (CBRSS, at http://www.cbrss.harvard.edu). Third, the Program in Foreign Policy Decision Making in the Department of Political Science at Texas A&M University (PFPDM, at http://www.polisci.tamu.edu/ForeignPolicy/index.html), founded in 1993, is focused on decision making in international relations and conflict resolution. It sponsors an Annual Winter Institute in Decision Theory, a colloquium series in Foreign Policy Analysis, advanced Workshops in Decision Making, and Graduate Student Conferences. The director of PFPDM is Alex Mintz. Finally, Minnesota's Center for the Study of Political Psychology (http://www.polisci.umn.edu/polipsyc), founded in 1995, sponsors a colloquium series as well as a number of collaborative research projects.

2.6 Books

It is beyond the scope of this article to detail the rich history of political psychology publications; interested readers might consult McGuire's (1993) and Ward's (2002) histories, which also include lists of classic books in political psychology, as well as Lerner's "Bibliographical Note" in Greenstein (1969). Political psychologists continue to publish books on specific substantive topics at an impressive rate, but my focus here is on general overview volumes that broadly review the central concerns of the field. An important mark of political psychology's intellectual legitimacy was the publication of the 1973 *Handbook of Political Psychology,* edited by Jeanne Knutson. Margaret Hermann edited a second "Handbook" (although that term is not part of the book's title), *Political Psychology* (1986). Both the Knutson and the Hermann handbooks were broadly concerned with a host of substantive, conceptual, and methodological issues in political psychology. Iyengar and McGuire's *Explorations in Political Psychology* (1993) served a similar function, although the emphasis in that volume is more narrowly focused on micro-level individual processes, such as attitudes, cognition and decision-making.[9] These three edited volumes, which targeted graduate students, academics, and practitioners, provide important documentation of the continuing development and evolution of the discipline.

The start of the 21st century has seen an upsurge in publication of books broadly concerned with political psychology, another indicator of the continued vitality of the field. In addition to previously noted third edition of the *Handbook of Political Psychology* (Sears, Huddy, and Jervis 2003), these include the volumes edited by Jim Kuklinski (2001, 2002), Kristen Monroe (2002), Victor Ottati et al (2002), Stanley Renshon and John Duckitt (2000), and Kawata and Araki (2003; this latter volume is in Japanese, but consists primarily of contributions by North American scholars).

All of the volumes mentioned in the preceding two paragraphs are best suited for graduate students, advanced undergraduates, and practicing political psychologists. There is a general consensus that the field has never really had a comprehensive undergraduate introductory text, and that is unfortunate. As Dana Ward recounts, "there is widespread agreement that the early texts, although useful, failed to adequately represent the discipline's diversity and did not capture the sense of excitement and utility that motivated the early political psychologists (an assessment that remains true today)" (2002: 67). Among the texts that have been used in introductory undergraduate courses are Barner-Barry and Rosenwein (1985), Elms (1976), Freedman and Freedman (1975), Stone (1976), Stone and Schaffner (1988), and the DiRenzo (1974) and Kressel (1993) anthologies.

All of these are out of print. Remarkably, given the enormous growth of the field in recent years, documented throughout this chapter, there has been no real progress in the development of undergraduate texts for political psychology, until very recently. A new comprehensive textbook, *Introduction to Political Psychology* (Cottam, Dietz-Uhler, Mastors, and Preston 2004) has just been published. Hopefully, this textbook (and even others to follow) will increase our ability to introduce the field of political psychology to large numbers of undergraduates on a regular basis. One plausible explanation for why political psychology has not been taught to more undergraduates is that an appropriate introductory textbook, updated periodically, did not exist.[10]

---

9   Lau and Sears' *Political Cognition* (1986) and Lodge and McGraw's *Political Judgment* (1995) are also edited volumes broadly concerned with individual-level cognitive processes.

10 An early reader of this chapter thought that I should "explain" why there is no undergraduate textbook in political psychology (again, a problem recently ameliorated by the Cottam et al. (2004) textbook). Based upon personal conversations I have had with publishing representatives, I would venture to say that it is *not* due to a lack of interest among publishers, who generally seem to recognize that a market exists. Rather, I suspect the absence is due to two features of political psychology per se. The first is that it is a

Finally, two book series are deserving of mention. The prestigious Cambridge University Press publishes a high profile series, titled "Studies in Political Psychology and Public Opinion." The series, under the general editorship of Jim Kuklinski and Dennis Chong, has quickly established itself as a leading outlet for political psychology scholarship. To date, the series has published 18 volumes, a number of which have won prominent disciplinary awards (in chronological order, the books in the Cambridge series are Sniderman, Brody, and Tetlock 1991, Zaller 1992, DeNardo 1995, Hibbing and Theiss-Morse 1995, Huckfeldt and Sprague 1995, Marcus, Sullivan, Theiss-Morse, and Wood 1995, Arian 1996, Mutz 1999, Lupia, McCubbins, and Popkin 2000, Hibbing and Theiss-Morse 2001, Kuklinski 2001, Welch, Sigelman, Bledsoe, and Combs 2001, Erikson, MacKuen, and Stimson 2002, Gibson and Gouws 2002, Hibbing and Theiss-Morse 2002, Kuklinski 2002, Huckfeldt, Johnson, and Sprague 2004, Stenner 2005). In addition, the *Research in Micropolitics* series, begun by Samuel Long and now under the editorship of Michael X. Delli Carpini, Leonie Huddy, and Robert Y. Shapiro, continues to publish essays on substantive and methodological importance to political psychology (volumes have been published in 1986, 1987, 1990, 1994, 1997, and 2003).

2.7 The Internet

The Internet plays a significant role in communication and the dissemination of information about political psychology. As I have taken care to document, most of the scholarly associations, training programs and workshops maintain homepages that provide internet-based information about their specific missions, as well as links to other resources that are helpful to political psychologists. ISPP, in particular, makes substantial use of the Internet in communicating with its members. The newsletter, *ISPPNews,* is transmitted electronically, and subscription, voting, and annual meeting activities can all be handled over the Internet. In addition to the resources I have already noted, two others are deserving of mention. First, ISPP and the Political Psychology Section of APSA maintain "POLPSYCH," the Political Psychology Internet Discussion Group, which is an automated public list used for rapid dissemination of

---

relatively small scholarly community, and so the pool of people who might be able (much less willing) to write such a text is limited. The second is that one of the key strengths of political psychology—pluralism in substance, theory, and method—makes writing such a text a rather daunting challenge, in order to fully capture the diversity and vitality of the field.

information. Subscription information is available at http://ispp.org/ISPP/polpsydis.html. Second, the International Bulletin of Political Psychology is a free electronic weekly newsletter published by Professor Richard Bloom of Embry-Riddle Aeronautical University that provides analysis of current events as well as information about a wide range of scholarly and practitioner activities. Information is available at http://security.pr.erau.edu.

2.8 Research Funding

Because political psychology is not a discipline in the traditional sense, it does not have unique sources of research funding. Rather, the granting agencies that fund basic research for the parent disciplines are the standard sources of research funding. The National Science Foundation (NSF), in particular the programs in the Directorate for Social, Behavioral, and Economic Sciences, has regularly funded social science research informed by a political psychological perspective. Of course, federal research dollars are scarce, and funding is competitive. Having had intensive, direct experience with the review process, I can say unequivocally that political psychology is *not* at a competitive disadvantage in the NSF review process. The same criteria hold as for any successful research proposal—the advancement of scientific knowledge, theoretical sophistication, and the rigorous use of appropriate empirical methodologies, all qualities that characterize the best political psychology research.

Survey research in particularly has been important in advancing the political psychological perspective, and NSF has been involved in funding many of the omnibus general population surveys that have been useful to political psychologists (including, but not limited to, the American National Election Survey, the General Social Survey, and the World Values Surveys). Two recent NSF initiatives that should be of interest to political psychologists are deserving of mention. First, an NSF-funded infrastructure project called *Time-sharing Experiments for the Social Sciences* (TESS) offers investigators, at no personal financial cost, an opportunity to test hypotheses via experimental survey methods (both telephone and internet-based) on large, diverse, randomly-selected subject populations (see http://www. experimentcentral.org for more details; Skip Lupia and Diana Mutz, the principle investigators, deserve credit for bringing TESS to fruition).

Second, the *Empirical Implications of Theoretical Models* (EITM) initiative at NSF, designed to integrate research utilizing positive political theory (formal modeling) and empirical analysis, deserves mention. I am aware that most political psychologists consider formal modeling to be antithetical to their research agendas, because positive political theory has traditionally been so closely linked to rational choice theoretical perspectives. However, there is no necessary link between formal modeling and a rational choice theoretical framework. As scholars who adopt a formal approach have slowly but surely come to accept the implications of empirical evidence that has shown that rational choice assumptions such as full information, expected utility maximization, and hyper-rationality are unrealistic, formal models have relaxed many of the standard general equilibrium assumptions and instead incorporated assumptions drawn from cognitive psychology. As a result, there have been several prominent attempts in the past decade to integrate positive political theory and behavioral psychological principles (see McGraw 2000, for a discussion). The NSF EITM initiative is an opportunity for political psychologists who are comfortable with this mode of scholarship to be involved with the synthesis of formal modeling and empirical analysis, which is sure to be a prominent, and well-funded, approach to political science scholarship in the new millennium.

In addition to funding from federal agencies, private foundations provide an additional source of funding for political psychology research. Among the private foundations that have recently funded political psychological research projects in various guises (with an example of their programmatic emphases in parentheses) are the Robert Wood Johnson Foundation (health), the Markle Foundation (communication and information technologies), the Pew Charitable Trusts (in particular, the Public Policy Program), the Russell Sage Foundation (work, immigration, and intergroup contact), the Spencer Foundation (education), and the Templeton Foundation (religion and spirituality).

Let me make a few closing comments about research funding, as it applies to some relatively unique facets of political psychology. Many scholars have argued that one of the defining elements of political psychology scholarship is the desire (on the part of practitioners) to make a difference in solving social and political problems by providing concrete policy recommendations (Deutsch and Kinnvall 2002, Hermann 1986). Certainly, research that improves societal welfare is more highly regarded by elected representatives and media pundits, and so it is an important criterion used in the broad distribution of federal research dollars (see Lupia 2000, and the accompanying articles for a thoughtful discussion of the "public value of political science research"). As a result, political psychological research might have a competitive advantage in the funding process, to the extent concrete policies and social problems are the focus. Unfortunately, being explicitly *political* can be a double-edged sword, as there is a natural tension in scholarly research between wanting to make a difference and adopting an objective, analytic, scientific perspective. Political psychologists may be particularly susceptible to charges that their conclusions are biased because their research is *not* value-neutral (see Tetlock 1994, and the attendant responses). There is no simple solution to the tension that exists between wanting to "do good" and being value-neutral, as well as the perception—warranted or not—that political psychological research may be more highly biased by ideological concerns than other social science perspectives. Because of the interdisciplinary and international character of the field, these issues become even more complex. Nonetheless, continued debate and reflection about the scientific practice of political psychology will be important if we are to maintain, or even increase, our influence on policy-making.

2.9 Concluding Thoughts

As a formal institution, political psychology is scarcely 30 years old, if we accept 1969 (the founding of the Yale Graduate Program), or 1973 (publication of the first *Handbook of Political Psychology)*, or 1978 (the establishment of ISPP) as rough indicators of the field's institutional date of birth. By most indications, its foundation is solid, and so it is well-poised to enter the new millennium with continued vitality and strength. The field's graduate programs and training institutes are strong, the scholarly associations are healthy, and an increased vitality in scholarship and publications is evident. The analysis of references in political science journals suggests that the political psychological perspective is having an increasing impact on the discipline, and there is every reason to believe that impact will continue to develop. Notably, ISPP has a history of systematically planning for its future, and in January of 2000, a workshop was held to develop a "Plan for the Third Decade of ISPP (2000-2010)," a well-thought out plan that has ramifications for the development of the field at large.

To this general rosy portrait of healthy growth and maturity, I would add two areas of concern. The first is the state of undergraduate education in political psychology. The subject matter of political psychology is intrinsically interesting to undergraduates, but we need to broaden the reach of political psychology at the undergraduate level. Reaching undergraduates is not only important for attracting the brightest minds of the younger generation into graduate programs in political psychology, but also for sensitizing the educated public at large to the value of our undertaking, an undertaking that will take on increased importance as policy makers grapple with the issues of intergroup conflict, terrorism, and a global economy in the 21st century.

Second, it is increasingly evident that political psychologists need to be actively involved in—indeed at the forefront of—the inevitable synthesis between positive political (rational choice) theory and behavioral approaches to judgment and decision making. Lupia and McCubbins (1998) is the prototypical example, but there are many others. Political psychologists need to be intimately involved with this emerging tradition, rather than leaving it to rational choice theorists or behavioral economists, because the fundamental basis of the enterprise is *our turf,* that is, psychological theories of judgment and decision making in the context of politics. The synthesis will occur, and it will be influential in political science, whether political psychologists are involved or not. This involvement will require three changes in political psychologists' orientation to their field. First, political psychologists need to accept a truce between the traditionally sniping factions (i.e., positive political theorists versus political psychologists of all stripes) and recognize the value of a formal approach to social science scholarship. Second, more political psychologists need to be trained in, and make use of, formal modeling techniques. Third, and most important, political psychologists need to be more forceful in bringing to the forefront their expertise in cognitive psychological principles, as well as the varied motivations (beyond self-interest) that characterize the human condition. This final point should make it clear that I am decidedly not calling for political psychologists to become rational choice theorists, but rather to become ever more vigorous in illustrating the fundamental limitations of the rational choice perspective. To the extent political psychology has influence on this emerging tradition in political science, its value and impact will become even more deeply entrenched in the discipline.

3 Personality Theory in the Analysis of Political Leadership: Trends, Schemas, and Opportunities

Elizabeth Marvick and Betty Glad

3.1 Early developments: Freud and the Repetition of Familial Adaptations

In classical psychoanalytic theory the propensity to transfer affect from infantile objects to other objects encountered in the course of life was assumed to be a fundamental mechanism shaping human psychodynamic structure. The operation of this process in a political context was the subject of one of the few models of psychopolitical behavior to be found in the work of Freud himself. In *Totem and Taboo* (1912) he used material from his medical practice and from the cultural anthropology of his day to explain certain myths and fetishistic practices in prehistory and in tribal societies.

In the next few years, some of Freud's followers would extend his theories to the study of modern political leaders. Ernest Jones contributed an essay on Louis Bonaparte (1913), Preserved Smith wrote on Martin Luther (1913), J. C. Flügel on Henry VIII (1920) and Leon C. Clark published essays on a series of political leaders, from Abraham Lincoln to Alexander the Great (1921, 1923).

While these first ventures into psychoanalytic study of political figures were mostly undertaken by historians or medical psychologists, Harold D. Lasswell utilized the theories to include contemporary political behavior of all kinds. Challenging a political science heavily weighted toward formal organizations and legal norms, he sketched the potential of psychoanalytic theory for understanding the development, structure and dynamics of personality-in-politics (see his "Types of Political Personalities" [1927] and *Psychopathology and Politics* [1930]). Thereafter, during a long career, Lasswell was to produce a series of works that touched on virtually every field of psychopolitical theory that has since been explored.

During World War II Lasswell led a group of political scientists (Nathan Leites, Alexander George, Ithiel Pool, Sebastian De Grazia) in the Department of Justice planning for psychological warfare campaigns against Hitler and other Axis leaders and their followers. This new kind of study, later continued in the Columbia University Center for the Study of Contemporary Cultures, was shaped by anthropological methods as well as psychoanalytic theory.

One of the first products of these projects was a study of Nazi personality traits as revealed in language patterns in official propaganda and other German communications (Leites and Kecskemeti 1947). The anthropologist Geoffrey Gorer did several studies on the Japanese, Burmese, and especially the Russian people (Gorer 1943, Gorer and Rickman 1949). In the Russian studies, dynamic patterns formed through childhood experience were seen as typical features of the adult Russian character. Building on this work, Nathan Leites delineated the personalities that shaped elite Bolshevik perspectives, beginning with the widely read *Operational Code of the Politburo* (1951), and still clearly visible in Leites's last publication, a second edition of his *Soviet Style in War* (1988).

This multidisciplinary approach spearheaded by Lasswell at first had little effect on most practitioners of traditional political science. But the appearance of *Woodrow Wilson* (1956), by Alexander George and Juliette George, marked a turning point. Written in an appealing narrative style this work offered a developmental explanation for just those aspects of Wilson's behavior—his moral arrogance and inability to compromise at critical junctures—that had been recognized as destructive of his professed aims. Wilson's plans for embedding a League of Nations Covenant in the peace treaty ending the first World War were defeated for "personal 'selfish' reasons" that caused him to refuse to collaborate with the United States Senate, and in particular, with the leader of its Foreign Relations Committee, Henry Cabot Lodge. The Georges show that this refusal continued a pattern of resistance that originated in Wilson's unconscious aggression toward his father who had humiliated and attempted to dominate him as a child (George and George 1956: 208).

Lasswell had anticipated that such studies, linking phases in psychic development to stages in physical maturation, might encounter "initial emotional difficulties" from more conventional fellow students of politics: "Some of the facts are not pretty and they are not the topics of polite conversation," he warned (Lasswell 1930: 14).

But "emotional difficulties" were not the only obstacle to Lasswellian analysis; more practical problems were also involved. Psychopolitical inquiry of this kind requires a form of "spiral" analysis. This is a progressive exchange of information on three dimensions of personality: developmental history, basic psychodynamic patterns, and relations within political context. This search for an explanation of unexpected leader behavior leads back to investigation of particular life experiences that help account for the anomaly. Identification of these, in turn, suggests revisions in understanding of the individual's psychodynamic patterns. Once such revisions are made, not only is certain political behavior better understood; other behavior, not previously noticed, is seen to be related and becomes salient, sending the investigator back to the subject's life history—and so on. By such continual exchange between personal history, psychodynamics and adult behavior, the personality of the leader emerges in increasingly understandable form.

This analytical process was routine for Lasswell whose subjects were patients in therapy. For others, however, obtaining data appropriate for the method often seemed problematical, particularly where intimate details on personal history were required. The Georges were able to obtain evidence on the humiliating treatment inflicted on Woodrow Wilson as a boy by his father from the testimony of witnesses and from "Wilson's own recollections of his...early fears that he was stupid, ugly, worthless and unlovable" (George and George 1956: 7f). Very rarely, extensive and intimate personal records of political leaders surface that throw light on important leaders' early experience. A unique record is the diary of Louis XIII's doctor, who recorded every move of his royal patient from his birth until the doctor's death when the king was twenty-eight and had ruled for eleven years. Until this manuscript was analyzed with the help of depth psychology, the political behavior of the French king had been considered "mysterious" and "contradictory," but its revelations made understandable his alternation between depression and energetic hard work, and between murderous self-assertion and abject dependency on the support and advice of his prime minister, Cardinal Richelieu. The diary also helped identify the sources of this ruler's predilection for warlike undertakings and certain other central policies of the regime (Marvick 1986).

Such sources of data are rare enough, but equally distracting to practitioners of more traditional methods was the early focus on subjects who exhibited highly neurotic, borderline, or even grossly pathological personalities. Thus Lasswell's *Psychopathology and Politics* (1930), aimed at showing how early experience shapes personality development and private motives are displaced onto public objects, focused on personal dysfunction, since his evidence was drawn mostly from case studies of analysands.

3.2 Ego-psychology and Self Psychology: Political Applications

Parallel with these developments, the expansion of psychoanalytic theory pointed to other ways in which dynamic psychology could be applied to political behavior. A new emphasis on the role of ego adaptation did not require attention to the bodily processes associated with instinctual conflict (Leites 1971), but addressed directly mechanisms of defense that were operative in everyday political life. Moreover, in looking at adaptive as well as maladaptive behavior, it countered the objections that previous studies were concerned only with pathology.

Anna Freud's monograph on the ego and its mechanisms of defense (1937), for example, focused on processes of normal development and was formulated in language that meshed easily with non-Freudian forms of social enquiry. Heinz Hartmann (Hartmann 1958) and some of his colleagues pointed a way toward analysis of the ego and its vicissitudes that did not depend on detailed penetration of the earliest inner conflicts of infant development nor of unconscious struggles that persisted throughout later stages of maturation.

Erik Erikson was gifted in presenting Freudian theory on infant development in terms that, if not "pretty," at least allowed discussion in "polite society." As Lucian Pye remarked of *Young Man Luther* (Erikson 1962), "Erikson does not aim for shock effects by juxtaposing psychoanalytical—hence highly private—matters and historical and religious matters." Instead, Pye wrote, his concept of ego-identity encompasses the individual's "cognitive processes and…information," as well as "his effective psychological defense mechanisms" and "his successful sublimations"—in short, every aspect of his adaptation to the choices that life presents (Pye 1961: 298). Increasingly directed toward progressive transformations of the ego in post-infantile years, Erikson's *Identity and the Life Cycle* (1959) was particularly germane to the interests in Indian political leadership of Suzanne Rudolph and Lloyd Rudolph, who were engaged in studying the development of democratic leadership in a traditional, hierarchical society (Rudolph and Rudolph 1967: 136-216). Erikson's own treatment of Gandhi (Erikson 1969), in turn, complemented theirs.

Most notably, ego psychology provided an expanded vocabulary for exploring narcissistic processes in leaders, processes that were coming to be regarded as increasingly central in the study of modern politics. Long-term trends that weakened traditional authority, and the subsequent decline, in western democracies, of effective party controls, have seen the ranks of political leadership increasingly dominated by self-recruited persons ready to offer their entire personality directly to the public for acceptance. As self-presentation of candidates and self-conducted campaigns for office have become the norm, very aggressive, narcissistic personalities have become more conspicuous in high office.

Thus Max Weber saw vanity and desire for power as characteristic of those who choose politics as a vocation, (Weber [1921] 1946: 116). Lasswell described a type of "agitators" who, "as a class" are "strongly narcissistic types." The opportunity to win gratifying feedback from large and admiring audiences helped to explain the attraction of this political role (Lasswell 1930:

10). The lure of politics for the narcissist is also, as Post notes, citing Volkan, that once power is gained, such a person "can actually restructure his reality" to conform to his needs (Post 1993: 109, Volkan 1980).

Lasswell was early aware of the varying ways in which narcissistic tendencies in the political leader worked themselves out in practice. For example, he perceived a benign outcome of Abraham Lincoln's narcissistic personality, with its "extreme demands for wide appreciation," in unifying the North in the long crisis that was marked by the American Civil War. The constructive effects of Lincoln's narcissism depended upon his ability to "hold his destructive impulses in sufficient restraint to permit him to coordinate the efforts of others in organization" (Lasswell 1936: 186-190). Volkan has distinguished the *destructive* type of narcissistic leader "who protects the cohesion of his grandiose self chiefly by devaluating others" from the *reparative* narcissistic national leader who "strengthens the cohesiveness and stability of his grandiose self by idealizing a group of others whom he then includes in an idealized extension of himself" (Volkan 1980).

The work of Heinz Kohut (Kohut 1991), also emphasizing positive as well as negative aspects of narcissistic adaptation, has informed several recent psychobiographies, including studies of Kaiser Wilhelm II (T. Kohut 1991), Abraham Lincoln (Strozier 1983), and Key Pittman (Glad 1986). Kohut's own treatment of Winston Churchill argues that the British wartime prime minister was able to channel the narcissistic adaptations manifest in his youth into aggression toward an evil enemy. With a passion derived from his own needs, and with commensurate oratorical skill, he transmitted to his followers the idealized image of a defiant fearless self leading a united and brave people against a wicked and ruthless foe. His passionate vision and his skill converted the ideal into a reality.

Kohut's analysis allows us to draw distinctions which are relevant to the problem of how a leader relates to others. Relationships of the narcissistic individual may confer the function of "mirror" upon the self-object. In this case the other is seen as returning the unconditional love and admiration in just those terms craved by the subject. Or the other may gratify the individual's hunger for an "ideal" self-object, representing the moral approval of an idealized father. The second motivational pattern, however, has most often been associated with a defeated or humiliated people's need to idealize a leader; it is unusual for a highly narcissistic leader to project his need for an ideal self-image onto a living figure. More recognizable is the "fantasized courage-supporting relationship" of the leader to God, or Providence, or perhaps an archaic national hero (Post 1993). Albert Speer testifies that Hitler identified with the hallowed image of Martin Luther. " 'Heretofore only one

German had been hailed like this: Luther,'" the German dictator exulted when he traveled about the country receiving the acclaim of the crowds. (Speer 1970: 105).

Neither George Washington nor Thomas Jefferson idealized any of their contemporaries as appropriate mentors or moral examples for themselves. George Washington's father had been little present in the home and died when his eldest son by a second marriage was eleven, leaving George to seek out father figures in a series of British military and civil commanders during his early military career on the western frontier (Marvick 2000: 88).

Time after time, as a young officer in the French and Indian war, Washington rode headlong into danger against unfavorable odds, as though he were challenging the gods to strike him down. In his letters of the time describing near-fatal military encounters, he reported the "miraculous" aspects of his survival as the work of "providence" (Washington 1983: 336-7). Risking his person and tempting fate in this way he acted like the gambler (which he actually also was, in a small way) who "dares to compel the gods to make a decision about him, hoping for their forgiveness," seeming to ask for "compensation or approval from the father" who had abandoned him (Fenichel 1945: 372). As he received ever more abundant evidence that he was blessed by providence he seems to have become more and more confident of paternal approval, a confidence signalled by his growing willingness to play the role of "father of his country." Jefferson, notoriously hostile to living authority figures, seems to have sometimes identified with a less secular high power: he edited his own version of the teachings of Jesus to demonstrate the consonance between his own morality and that of the Christian God (Jefferson 1983).

A frequently found relationship is the narcissistic leader's exaltation of his followers—the "people," "public opinion," the "common man" or "posterity"—as an all-knowing and singularly virtuous source of his power. Scattered throughout the papers of both Washington and Jefferson is evidence of their expectation that their leadership will be vindicated by the approval of generations to come.

In contrast with a narcissistic dynamic that has relatively "benign," "reparative" or "constructive" effects is the "malignant" or "destructive" narcissist, exemplified by such aggressive tyrants as Hitler (Langer [1943] 1972, Waite 1977), and Stalin (Tucker 1973). These pariahs of modern times were persons with high levels of rage, tendencies to picture the world as split between loathsome and pure objects, and failure to develop super ego controls. Abundant testimony from intimates (Alliluyeva 1967, Speer 1970), as well as specialized assessments (Bromberg and Small 1983), indicated gross pathologies along these lines in Hitler and Stalin. Further work remains to be done on how family experience helps to explain these differences in the psychodynamic structures of the benign as contrasted to the more malignant, paranoid types of leaders and the particular destructive political forms taken by the latter types (Robins and Post 1997: 17, Glad 2002b). As Blema Steinberg has shown, however, expression of narcissistic needs in destructive behavior is by no means confined to the leaders of authoritarian systems or to the patently pathological (Steinberg 1996). Nevertheless, if a variety of personality types are found in every society, the political system itself tends to reward some over others to maintain its stability. Moreover, any system may call for different personality characteristics in a leader depending upon the stage of processes within it tending to reform or transformation.

3.3 Leader Personalities in the Context of Regime Characteristics

It is evident that the personality traits valued in political leaders will vary according to the state of the regime. At times, when systems have collapsed or are in stasis, different personality types may come to the top. The discussion that follows is a preliminary attempt to synthesize and systematize some of the covariations that have been observed.

The relationship between a type of regime and the type of leaders apt to be chosen was noted by Alexis de Tocqueville (1874: 155). It seemed to him that the morally elevated, autonomous leaders who had transformed the American colonies into a democratic system three generations before had been succeeded, in his time, by men who were weakly subservient to the vagaries of public opinion.

Consistently with Tocqueville's view, Berger argues that "people who try to acquire power in democracies" show "a notable narcissistic fragility and an excessive need for ascendancy" (Berger 1993: 24). The hypothesis is that grandiosity and intense demand for public approval distinguish the personality type that seeks power in modern democratic systems. Indeed, mistrust of such self-aggrandizement has been held to explain resistance in some hierarchical folk societies of Africa to democratic methods: "Rural inhabitants professed uneasiness about a foreign system...which encourages the un-African vice of personal ambition by enabling all to put themselves forward unasked and to agitate through the villages without seeking the leave of the chiefs" (Mackenzie and Robins 1960: 266-7).

Still, without further research, an opposing hypothesis might seem equally plausible. For example, the unbridled competition characteristic of democratic regimes, and the greater constriction in them of opportunities for a single person to gratify grandiose designs, might actually discourage excessively narcissistic persons from seeking political leadership positions. At the very least, such constriction might be expected to change such persons' preferred path to political eminence from ascent on the political ladder (e. g., party, pressure group, bureaucracy) to lateral access from the entertainment or business world.

The tasks of individual leaders in regimes that are in transition from traditional or authoritarian orders to more democratic polities, are especially difficult and are apt to call for a distinctive type of leader. Those who rise to such challenges are likely to be those who can assume heroic roles, seeing themselves as possessing exceptional vision and leadership capabilities.

Often the men who undertake leadership of such revolutions have grandiose and destructive proclivities: The "tragic feature of revolutions," as Ernest Jones suggests, is that their leaders "tend to reproduce just the attributes of their predecessors against which they had most vehemently inveighed." The overturned authority represents, he speculated, the father whom one wishes to replace "with the object of reigning in his stead in the same fashion...and with his same attributes" (Jones 1951: 261). Once the father has been destroyed, the angry son rules in his place. Thus it often happens, as a later psychoanalyst, Charles Brenner, concludes, that "yesterday's foe of tyranny becomes today's tyrant." Usually, in this interpretation, revolutionists "are motivated by an unconscious wish to become like the very rulers they consciously detest (Brenner 1974: 225-228).

Support for this view is provided by E. V. Wolfenstein's (1967) study of Lenin, Trotsky, and Gandhi in the light of their differing father-son relationships in early years He suggests that the less conflictual and the better resolved these relationships had been, the less destructive were the consequences of the leader's revolutionary success.

This pattern is exemplified by the sequence of events that unfolded in France after 1789, as former champions of the people became their oppressors, reenacting the classical scenario of a family tragedy in so many details that it may have provided the prototype for Freud's reflections, as it did generations later to the historian Lynn Hunt (1992).

The tyrants of the twentieth-century who have ruled outside the law and brought misery and destruction to their own people and others all had harsh fathers in their background. The "malignant narcissists"—Stalin, Hitler, and Saddam Hussein, for example—used their power to wreak vengeance on a continually expanding assortment of enemies and, for the sake of their own survival, to vent their rage on their own people as well (Glad 2002b, Post 1993).

What is interesting is that there are notable uniformities in the narcissistic processes at work in these malignant personalities: all seem to have failed to form early attachments to nurturing figures—a precondition for empathy and trust. In the maturation process, they failed to establish a basic sense of self-worth and coherence that makes possible consistent, realistic relations with the outside world. As compensation, all formed grandiose ideas of themselves as omnicompetent and omnipotent. All had strongly paranoid tendencies and lacked inhibitions against extreme cruelty, acting out their sadistic impulses against others who represented to them bad aspects of themselves (Glad 2002b, Post 1993, Robins and Post 1997).

Still, not all revolutionary leaders follow this pattern. In some cases the cyclical pattern of events—idealistic revolutionary leader-into-oppressive-tyrant—fits very imperfectly with the history and dynamics of a revolution. This seems to be the case with leaders of the American revolution. Though Burrows and Wallace (1972) attempted to fit the American revolutionary movement into the "classic" model, another historian of that revolution suggests that the relations of the Patriot leaders with their fathers were less conflictual than those of their counterparts on the Loyalist side (Lynn 1977). In short, the classical model fits poorly with the "transformational" "benign" revolutionary figures of the nascent American republic.

Leaders in other polities have accomplished even greater changes without employing repressive measures against their own people. Mohandas Gandhi was one of these. Gandhi's leadership (not as head of state but as "teacher" or guide) has been taken as an example of the transformation of narcissistic processes into policies with the benign intent of peacefully enhancing popular liberties and expanding, rather than restricting, participation in the exercise of power. A variety of authors have identified different stages in Gandhi's personal development as critical to this transformation (e.g.,Wolfenstein 1967, Rudolph and Rudolph 1967, Erikson 1969, J. M. Burns 1978: pp. 90-92, Blanchard 1984).

Mustafa Kemal, too, led a Turkish revolution whose "destructive aspects" were "very much under control." By channeling his own ambitions and energy into creating a modernized Turkey, Kemal included the Turkish people and his own idealized self in the same embrace of narcissistic illusion. In doing so he secured the supplies of affection and admiration he craved, but at the same time he made palpable improvements in the lives of those who supplied them (Volkan 1980, Volkan and Itzkowitz 1984).

Mikhail Gorbachev sought reform and the dispersal of authority within the Soviet system, adopting a policy of incrementalism to achieve that end. De Klerk and Mandela of South Africa were also able to control their grandiose ambitions sufficiently to collaborate in achieving a radical transition in their common country via peaceful means rather than violent ones (Glad 1996).

To develop a more differentiated theory of the relationships of personality to transformational leadership, one might compare the relatively benign leaders to each other and analyze the significance of certain characteristics that differentiate them from their malignant counterparts.

Thus, George Washington and Mustafa Kemal were both professional soldiers before they became revolutionary leaders, able to put highly controlled ambitions for their countrymen to work on behalf of ideals of mutual respect and shared power. The military vocation of Idi Amin, on the other hand, was a prelude to his murderous tyranny in Uganda. Variations in the quality of this common career experience might be examined for clues to the vast differences in outcomes.

Parallels are also evident between the political roles played by George Washington and Nelson Mandela. Each of these two "founders" demonstrated, in the long revolutionary struggle as well as afterward, a cautious, yet firm moderation, self-conscious efforts to model an example of respect for diversity and civil liberties, and a pattern of conspicuous renunciation of personal power. Washington and Mandela both declined to perpetuate themselves in office when offered the opportunity to do so. These commonalities in leadership aims and style suggest that there may be other parallels in psychic development and dynamics of these two leaders, despite the great difference in their cultural formation. And in fact, comparing the backgrounds of the last two men brings out other similarities that could be further explored. Like Mandela, Washington was the first son of his mother. Like him too, he, his mother, and his younger siblings formed his father's "B-team." (In Mandela's case his mother was the third wife of his father, in Washington's, the second.) Both experienced the frequent absence and early death of fathers; both had elder half siblings with prior entitlements to their fathers' legacies (Marvick 2000, Sampson 1999: 1-15, Meredith 1998: i).

The vision that Washington formed of a state without hereditary distinctions in which citizens enjoyed equal rights was forged when as a youth he suffered slights from British officers that evoked family experiences of his childhood. His impatience, anger and rebelliousness were transformed, partly through providential military successes, into the personality of the "founding father"—perhaps an idealized version of the father whom he had hardly known. This hard-won self-confidence enabled him to represent to his new country the benign and even-handed leadership he had wished for himself and his brothers-in-arms.

As for Mandela, he suffered the sting of an even more serious discrimination in his early adult career, but as a child of royal background, he seems to have had the self-esteem that enabled him to surmount what could have been serious psychic wounds. Certainly his long years of self-controlled energetic activity under isolated conditions of extreme hardship, his conciliatory stance vis-à-vis those responsible for his confinement, and his realistic adaptations to political and economic facts in forging a workable compromise in the transfer of power, are all signs of consistent and gratifying nurturing in earliest childhood and later experiences that helped him to develop a profound sense of self-worth and a capacity for self-control.

Still, there is other evidence that positive early nurturing need not always be a condition of benign leadership. Mustafa Kemal's motivation in expanding the liberties of the Turkish people while minimizing the destructive consequences of radical change, has been ascribed by Volkan to his early experience with a mother incapable of forming a close and gratifying relationship with her son. His motivation for creating an autonomous Turkey and radically reforming, with a strong though relatively benign hand, its political system, was a grandiose and idealized self-conception, partly the legacy of his emotionally ungratifying childhood, that propelled him to "repair" his own deprivation in the national arena (Volkan 1980). The puzzle here is what enabled him, unlike Stalin or Hitler, to adopt a relatively constructive role.

More differentiated analysis is also stimulated by the fact that more benign leaders may manifest, to a lesser degree, some of the personality traits evident in the malignant types. Work on Charles de Gaulle, for example (Leites 1977), Mustafa Kemal, (Volkan and Itzkowitz 1984), and Richard Nixon (Volkan, Itzkowitz, and Dod 1997, Steinberg 1996: 181-205), are useful beginnings along these lines. Though the behaviors of these leaders differ greatly in essentials from those ascribed to tyrants who "go too far" (Glad 2002b), they all share some psychodynamic patterns that, in the malevolent autocrats, took a pathologically destructive form. Volkan writes that Kemal, just before his death, gave "some evidence that he had begun to lose his grip on his grandiose self and that he had become irritable and rather suspicious" (Volkan 1980). Charles de Gaulle, successful symbol of the liberation of France and founder and longtime leader of a transformed and democratic state, nevertheless showed a narcissistic tendency not only to exalt the French nation by attributing to it qualities of his idealized self, but also to project onto the French people aspects of his "bad" self: France was alternately depicted as glorious and independent or degraded and dragged through the "mud" (Leites 1977: 151-63).

Thus, such "splitting" in object relations, so characteristic of oppressive rulers, may appear in a minor key in democratic leaders. Ronald Reagan saw the battle between the United States and the Soviet Union in black and white terms, in which evil was attributed to the latter (Glad 1983). Traits bordering on the paranoid were observed in George Washington (Knollenberg 1968).

Perhaps this problem will be resolved by identifying a cluster of deeply embedded traits, expressed in a system that permits their relatively free acting out, that differentiate the potentially destructive leader from his more constructive counterpart. Glad's work on the psychological history of the tyrant (2002b) suggests that this may be the case. The aim of such study is to advance toward a differential "diagnosis" that helps explain which motives will be operative in which kinds of cases.

3.4 Leadership style

A leader's style is the behavioral pattern in which he addresses himself to others and to his tasks. It includes modes of processing information, self-presentation to others and interaction with them, and ways of making decisions. James D. Barber, in his study of Presidential character, has called style "the most visible part" of the personality pattern. One dimension of leadership style, as he sees it, is *"activity -passivity"*—the energy the leader brings to the role (Barber 1985: 4-11). In applying this measure, Barber locates the American President Eisenhower toward the passive end of the continuum, showing a propensity for "withdrawal, for moving away from conflict and detail" (Barber: 148).

In his work on Eisenhower, however, Fred Greenstein has seen a "hidden hand" style in Presidential leadership. Eisenhower, he argues, preferred indirection to confrontation, behind-the-scenes manipulation to open domination. Typical were his tactics of deflecting criticism by addressing a press conference with a few "bumbling" remarks, then instructing his aide to step in to represent his policy as pending, impersonal, or deferred altogether (Greenstein 1982). The tactics were clearly adaptive in terms of Eisenhower's political career. He had an exceptional record for winning bi-partisan support for policies while sustaining his own popularity. This adaptation, we argue, was not only effective. It was also deeply rooted in his personality. In a revealing memoir, his salient recollections of childhood terrors are of fearful efforts at self-defence. Once he intervened on behalf of his older brother, physically confronting his father who, his face "black as thunder" was beating the older boy with a harness tug. He reports that, to his surprise, when his father "turned on me" he suffered no punishment (Eisenhower 1967: 40-44). Seemingly, he had expected the worst—perhaps destruction—from his bold challenge.

Eisenhower's consciousness of his problems in controlling his own aggression and explosive temper seems likely to be related to the sensations he reports in recalling his boyhood. Mixed with his anger, apparently, was a deeply inhibiting fear of the damage his rage might wreak on himself or the other.

Further examination of Eisenhower's personal history shows that his choice of and persistence in a military vocation—certainly a choice that affords means for channeling destructive impulses in socially approved directions—was marked by considerable ambivalence throughout his career (Eisenhower 1967). Moreover, certain of his policy choices, as for example his decision not to proceed with the American armies to occupy Berlin as the German forces were retreating during World War II, may have reflected personal ambivalence as well as strategic considerations. Conflict, sometimes intense, between aggressive and pacific action plans, between violent and non-violent strategies, is a personality characteristic he exhibited in a wide variety of contexts.

Eisenhower's style as chief executive may be likened to that of two other American Presidents. As Todd Estes claims "Washington displayed nearly all the hallmarks of what scholars have termed the hidden-hand presidency: the delegation of tasks to others, the use of personality, the instrumental use of language to send signals…and the development of broad-based support that transcends normal political divisions." Estes's evidence is based on a case study of Washington's methods in securing ratification of the treaty with Britain negotiated by John Jay in 1794. Before submitting the treaty to the Senate Washington set the stage behind the scenes by marshalling press support for it through a variety of proxies without divulging his own position in public (Estes 2001: 156).

Thomas Jefferson also made a practice of "hiding his hand." To intimates he would express murderous thoughts, as when he declared to a young protégé, in his famous "Adam and Eve" defense of the Terror in France, that rather than have seen the French Revolution fail "I would have seen half the earth desolated," or when he expressed aggressive impulses toward George Washington, under whom he was serving as Secretary of State. During that period he wrote to his intimate, James Madison, that support of a branch of the United States Bank in Virginia, which Washington sponsored, "is an act of *treason* against the state," and that whosoever acted as an agent of the bank should "be adjudged guilty of high treason and suffer death accordingly" (Jefferson 1950-: v24: 433, v25: 143). As Vice President under John Adams he secretly subsidized scurrilous press attacks on the President and rejoiced in them privately, saying "I think I see John Adams twirling off his wig and stamping on it!" *(Richmond Recorder* 1802).

Yet once in office he was notoriously non-confrontational. As governor of Virginia during the Revolution he was nominally in charge of that state's resistance to British incursions, yet his tactics were confined to writing hopeful letters of direction to all and sundry and were so ineffective that one general warned him, "an Army on paper will give you no security." A biographer comments "Perhaps that was one of his failings—the belief that dispatching a letter could solve a situation" (Schachner 1951: 214). As President he was equally nonconfrontational in his tactics, charming visitors of all persuasions by seeming to agree with their positions (Marvick 1997a). He declined to appear before Congress in person on almost all occasions, operating indirectly through party agents in the legislature and press. His choice of policies of indirection—such as demilitarization and embargo—"brought the country to a situation where war was impossible...and peace was only a name for passive war" (Adams 1986: 1082).

Despite the commonalities in leadership style among these three American presidents, the psychodynamic patterns laid down in their widely diverging personal histories deserve further study. In some ways Washington and Eisenhower were alike. Both engaged in risky, aggressive action in their youth—Washington as a young officer fighting the French in the western wilderness, Eisenhower as a wholly engaged, ambitious football player at West Point Academy (with self-damaging results). Both faced the problem, during their careers, of controlling potentially explosive rage, a factor contributing to the indirect methods of political control that they sometimes chose to employ.

Still, there were important differences between these two men. The inhibition of rage associated with Washington's non-confrontational style was achieved without the signs of fear and guilt shown by Eisenhower's account of his own personality problems. There is no evidence that the first president's mastery of his hot temper caused any further conflict in his later years, whereas Eisenhower continued to complain of the problem and to seek strategies to control it. Eisenhower sometimes somatized his conflicts. Washington did not.

In short, Eisenhower's avoidance of confrontation in leadership probably served as a defense against unconscious fears, as well as a deliberate strategy to affect policy outcomes. This made it more difficult for him to change his style when strategic needs seemed to call for direct leadership, as, for example, in dealing with issues of civil rights, or the depredations of Joseph McCarthy. Washington, on the other hand, was more than willing to present himself personally to influence policy, when it seemed needed. On one historic occasion Washington assumed an heroic stance, confronting a rebellion in the American army and facing it down. Estes's account of his tactics in securing the ratification of the Jay treaty show that after covertly setting the scene by using proxies in the press to rally public opinion, he assumed personal leadership in the move for ratification and confronted the House of Representatives with a direct refusal when it claimed a right to review the record of the negotiations that had led to the treaty: "A just regard to the Constitution... forbids a compliance with your request," he told them flatly (Estes 2001: 151). And, once he became convinced that an insurrection against whiskey excise taxes in western Pennsylvania threatened the national union, he prepared to lead a military campaign in person to suppress it.

What this suggests is that depth psychology may alert us to subtle differences at the stylistic level that might otherwise go unnoticed. If our analysis is correct, Eisenhower did not have as wide a choice of options as did George Washington, when faced with the need to "sell" a policy to Congress or the public. Unconscious processes of the kind here attributed to Eisenhower cannot as easily be adapted to the service of the ego when contextual demands change. Washington's striking stylistic flexibility, by way of contrast, seems founded on more effective resolution of earlier personal conflicts, a flexibility that he employed both in combating enemies of his republican ideals and constructing the new state that would support those aims.

3.5 Developments for the Future: Leaders in Context

As suggested in the foregoing section, the potentiality for enhancing the value of personality theory in the analysis of political leadership lies not only in developing ever more discriminating descriptions of personality—its etiology, structure and dynamics—but also in juxtaposing these findings with the ways in which leaders define their goals, relate to others and adapt to selected aspects of the political environment. Promising work, as the following suggests, has already been taken in terms of several kinds of relationships.

3.5.1 Interrelations of Leaders

A relatively new line of inquiry that promises to be productive involves analysis of the interactions between leaders. One may look, for example, at leadership pairs in terms of their ability to co-operate in the pursuit of their goals. A peaceful transformation is most likely when the leaders of the old order and the leaders of the new order can work together, each side holding back the extreme of the political spectrum which he represents (Glad 1996). The difficulties that Mikhail Gorbachev had in transforming the Soviet Union were due in part to the fact that Boris Yeltsin undercut his efforts to bring the

Communist Party along with him. Directly challenging the status and values of the Communist Party leadership, Yeltsin indirectly contributed to the desperation that fed the coup attempt that occurred in 1991. The cooperation between William de Klerk and Nelson Mandela in South Africa, by way of contrast, enabled that nation to avoid a crisis of this order. De Klerk was able to bring elements of the National Party and Afrikaner population along with him because Mandela pledged himself to a policy in which whites and blacks would work together. Each man held back the extremes in the part of the populace which he led (Glad 1999, 1996).

Earlier life experience contributed to these inclinations toward cooperation or competition. Yeltsin, the only one known to have had a childhood experience of physical conflict with his father, was the one most prone to court risks to himself in his drive for power. He had a history of having triumphed satisfactorily as an early adolescent in standing up to his father, in winning redress from a primary school teacher who he believed had treated him unjustly, and in seeing the teacher punished according to the rules. When he triumphed over Gorbachev he exacted retribution and showed a proclivity toward sadistic revenge (Glad 1996).

Another exceptional case of collaborative intra-group leadership relations played out relatively benignly not only in the struggle to establish independence for the American colonies, but also in framing the basic laws of the new republic and in directing its policy for the next three decades. The actors in this American movement—those who took a leading part at every stage in the establishment of the new nation—comprised as few as a dozen leaders, and among these was a distinctive nucleus of only five or six closely interrelated Virginian plantation owners, Washington, Jefferson, Madison, John Marshall, Edmund Randolph and James Monroe. This smaller, provincial core emerged from the larger, regionally diverse group to preside over the national scene for three decades, holding posts of dominance out of all proportion to their numbers. Their common family experiences and other cultural and material determinants of early formation seem to have resulted in commonalities of personality, perspective and behavior that enabled them to sustain these leading positions for so long a time (Marvick 2002).

In these settings all seem to have enjoyed an early childhood exceptionally free from physical restrictions and exceptionally indulgent in the satisfaction of nurturing needs. This helps to account for the signs each exhibited of a personality with a low level of rage. Their infantile needs were supplied by multiple caretakers, so that their first steps toward maturity were usually taken in the presence of several others. Moreover, they were served from infancy by slave companions near their own age, as well as older nurses, all formally subordinate to themselves.

Preliminary results of a study tracing the impact of these common elements on later political functioning of the Virginian leaders are these: despite the narrow provincial character of their early experience, their narcissistic needs were channeled into self-images of autonomous, free-thinking, rational republicans, holding ideals consonant with the European Enlightenment. Their formal superiority to most of their early intimates had encouraged them to conceive that pursuing their political ambitions was the performance of an honorable duty in the service of these ideals. In the setting in which they were raised their world was literally a stage, surrounding them with spectators. As the performers on that stage, they were rehearsed to apprehend and adapt to their audience, depending upon whether it comprised elder or younger kin and neighbors, or—in much larger numbers—servants of radically lower status and diverse ages and functions.

After the military service they all performed—at least nominally—during the Revolutionary War, their ideological positions began to diverge, but all directed their ambitions toward the national arena, in contrast with many of their Virginian counterparts who preferred retirement or purely local distinctions. All these "founders" became adept in analyzing national opinion and in manipulating it skillfully. All showed, in their political performances, exceptional flexibility in choosing tactics to implement their aims. This adaptive capacity also enabled them to maintain their various political bases, even when their private ideological positions differed significantly from those of their constituents.

Other work delineates the sources of both conflicts and co-operation in the collaborative actions of the Allied leaders during World War II. F.D. Roosevelt's need to conceive of himself as the master-puppeteer of the entire Allied strategy—as in assuring his military chiefs that "the United States has the whip hand" in its conflict with the British over De Gaulle's role—was the source of his efforts to prevent De Gaulle from playing any part whatever in the war. For his part, De Gaulle saw himself as equal to Roosevelt and Churchill in that effort. He also proved completely impervious to Roosevelt's charm, seeing that the American leader wanted France to "recognize him as its savior and arbiter" (Dallek 1979: 376-379). Roosevelt found this insufferable. Loewenheim (1975) argues that the president's demands on Churchill to exclude De Gaulle were humiliating to the British leader, as well as detrimental to the allied military collaboration. It would have been still more detrimental had not Churchill usually been willing to subordinate himself to the American leader in the service of his own supreme aims. Roosevelt's need to believe in the power of his personal charm sometimes led even to attempts to exclude Churchill from proposed meetings with Stalin, whom he had not yet met. He wrote to the prime minister before the Yalta meeting, "I know that you won't hold it against me if I tell you with brutal frankness that I am personally better able to manage Stalin than you are...He is persuaded that he prefers me and I hope he will continue thus" (Loewenheim et al. 1975: 196, Senarclens 1984: 19).

3.5.2 Leaders and Advisers

The interaction between leaders and those who advise or otherwise influence them has long been a central object of research into personality and politics (Goldhamer 1978). The psychoanalytical literature we have reviewed here provided a framework for understanding the operative psychic mechanisms—e.g., transference, projection, identification—through which the role of the aide in some way comes to seem to the principal a representation of himself. The personal, or affective, function played by a certain kind of adjunct to the leader—the "favorite"—was early made the object of study as it was found in the courts of early modern Europe (Marvick 1983).

In modern American history Woodrow Wilson's relationship to Colonel House is instructive. That president is reported to have said of this relationship, "Mr. House is my second personality. He is my independent self" (Freud and Bullitt 1966: 45). Indeed, House's ability to preserve his powerful role of principal adviser to the President was maintained for seven years by his self-discipline in convincing Wilson of his complete selflessness. The relationship finally ruptured when House's disagreements with the president on policy weakened this self-discipline. Wilson felt himself betrayed by these signs of independence and suspected his adviser of rivalrous ambition (George and George 1956: 128-132).

More recent studies have continued to elaborate on how advisers may relate to their principals in a variety of positive as well as negative ways. The services aides provide for the leader range all the way from the alter ego that Wilson first conceived Colonel House to be, to simple agents or deputies with purely instrumental roles. In between are those who bolster the leader's self confidence, compensate for some of his vulnerabilities (i.e., use anger on his behalf, promote order in a chaotic decision-making process, or act as a proxy, doing things for their principal that he wishes to disown, either psychologically or politically). At times, aides on whom the leader is particularly dependent may perform as strategic actors, shaping the principal's ways of thinking to orient him towards an agenda they favor or to contribute to orderly decision making (Glad and Link 1996).

Jimmy Carter is an American president whose advisers' psychic functions for him ranged from instrumental service (Cyrus Vance, Stuart Eizenstat) to affective interactions involving approval and mirroring (Rosalynn Carter, Patrick Caddell). At times these affective interactions simply provided Carter with the emotional support requisite to high-level functioning in a stressful situation (e.g., Vance and Rosalynn Carter at Camp David). At other times some aides were strategic actors, pushing their own agendas on the President. Patrick Caddell, for example, convinced Carter that he should deliver his famous "malaise" speech by suggesting to him that he would thus become a moral leader like Woodrow Wilson. The Vice President Walter Mondale and Hamilton Jordan, both of whom had serious reservations about another speech on energy, were sidelined on this issue (Link and Glad 1994). In pushing the tilt towards a security relationship with China, Zbigniew Brzezinski utilized his extraordinary access to Carter, as well as his bureaucratic skills, to create a momentum for a policy that he, Brzezinski, favored. He persuaded Carter to go along with his plans, in part, by suggesting that "standing tough" vis à vis the Soviet Union would promote one of the President's highest priority items, the successful conclusion and ratification of the Salt 2 Treaty (Glad 2003b).

While such affective ties, and their relationship to leader performance, are of central importance for the study of politics, certain factors have tended to restrict the attention they have received in psychopolitical research. One reason for this is that the leader-aide relationship is often deliberately made obscure. In discussing Colonel House's efforts to conceal his importance in Wilson's counsel, Goldhamer relates that House's role was "paralleled in England by that of Maurice Hankey who was so self-effacing that "when House...made contact with all the British leaders he thought important, he was ignorant of Hankey's role in the government" (Goldhamer 1978: 114). A second reason for this relative neglect may be due to a tendency to overrate the autonomy of leaders, especially elected leaders. This tendency is amplified when the principal is popular, energetic and intelligent. And, of course, if these qualities are lacking, the motives of the leader's entourage to conceal that fact, and the nature of their own roles as well, are further multiplied.

3.5.3 Leaders and Followers

The nature of the affective tie between the leader and his more distant followers is a productive subject of inquiry. The charismatic leader, for example, seems to be godlike—a person with powers that will work magic on behalf of his followers—and human—one with whom they can identify. In Max Weber's description, such a person is "treated as endowed with supernatural, superhuman, or at least specifically exceptional . . . qualities . . . regarded as of divine origin or as exemplary" (Weber 1947: 358-9). Consistently with this, Irvine Schiffer suggests that "charisma" is an attribute of "popular imagery" and pertains to the "psychology of the subject who views the phenomenon" (Schiffer 1973: 11, 19). It is not an attribute of the leader, but of the follower. Thus, the vast literature on public response to charismatic leaders is largely outside the scope of our concerns here.

Nevertheless, the relationship between leader and follower is comprised partly of leader behavior and personality. Heinz Kohut's work is useful in understanding the psychodynamic aspects of such a relationship. For the charismatic leader, the public may serve a mirroring function, convincing him that he is as great as he presents himself as being. Such gratification may reflect the public's experience of fusion with the leader. His power, his courage is theirs.

Inquiry into these types of relationships has been facilitated by studies of patient-therapist sessions or other forms of the depth interview (Lasswell 1930, Lane 1962). Sebastian De Grazia's study of Chicago analytic patients' responses to the death of Franklin Roosevelt (De Grazia 1945) was the first to document how the image of a president is internalized by some members of his public as representing a family member from their own past. Greenstein (1968) has discussed possibilities and methodological problems in collecting and using such data for psychopolitical research (see also M. Lerner, in Greenstein 1969).

Other studies suggest that adolescents were the age group most stricken by the death of President Kennedy in 1963; Martha Wolfenstein (1965) hypothesized that adolescents expressed their conflicted feelings toward their own young parents by transforming them into intense and prolonged mourning for the slain father figure, the President. Building on this work, David Sears argues that the extreme hostility to Lyndon Johnson shown by many highly educated, liberal young adults in 1968 and after was "anger toward any replacement person;" Lyndon Johnson was "seen as a usurper" (Sears 2002: 262-4). These responses of the public were certainly affected by the imagery projected, involuntarily or deliberately, by each president. The projection was, in turn partly a function of each one's personality.

Analyses along the foregoing lines may illuminate further the nature of the personality affinities and hostilities between leader and led that were evident during the Clinton presidency. What accounts for the fact that some persons discounted the importance of the sexual scandals for that presidency? Was there a comparable factor at work in the exaggerated hostility—even deep rage—that seems to have inspired some of those who persisted in opposing him despite his continued popularity? How are congruent, or incongruent projection patterns, based on common or unlike early experience a factor in leader-follower interaction? (Glad 2003a)

A barrier to this kind of research, according to the social psychologist, G. V. Caprara, is that "politicians are not generally directly accessible to students of personality" because they are often "reluctant to comply with the standard assessment procedures" that he and like investigators administer to large samples of the public (Caprara 2001). Nor has most survey research into political opinion been very useful. Many of such attitude studies fail to tap attitudes towards top political leaders that would be of much use to those employing depth-psychological analysis. Even when samples are said to be controlled for "demographics," as in a recent study of congruence between politicians' and public's personal traits (Caprara, Barbaranelli, and Zimbardo 2002), they ignore some obvious variables. To rectify this problem survey instruments could be devised to collect information on such matters as birth order, sibling distribution, gender, and parental marital status. Enquiries on such demographics would not be seen as too intrusive, all the while providing data and cues for more detailed follow-up interviews.

3.5.4 Differential Adaptations to Crises

Crisis situations, as Holsti (1990) has pointed out, are apt to reduce the leader's "ability to review the major options and assess the most relevant information." The result is likely to be an increase in "cognitive rigidities" and "stereotypic thinking."

At the time of the Iranian hostage crisis in 1979, for example, Jimmy Carter approved a highly risky operation to secure release of those held. Failing directly to address the high possibility of a failure and its likely consequences, he set up a meeting in which he stated his strong personal predilection for rescue. With his Secretary of State away for a short vacation, the only person who might have challenged him was not present. The result was that the President and members of the group together reconfirmed the President's known preferences in the virtual absence of criticism or dissent (Glad 1989). "Groupthink " as such mutual reinforcement has been called by Janis (1972) served to channel "tunnel vision" in policy choice, shutting out dissonant views and further hastening a high risk venture without adequate preparation.

Adaptations along these lines are visible in the response of some American leaders to the shattering events of September 11, 2001. Words emanating from the national administration in the next few hours and days tended to converge on stereotypes ("this is 'War' ") rather than analysis, and to suggest simplified, noninstrumental strategies to avoid confronting the crisis (such as retreat into the family circle, resuming "normal" everyday patterns of life).

Crisis situations, however, do not always lead to simplistic thinking and consensus seeking. Franklin D. Roosevelt, for example, taking office in 1933 at a time of deep national financial crisis, broadcast simple mass appeals containing sloganized reassurances. Yet the president himself was notoriously open to a wide variety of strategies to cope with the unfolding challenges. Far from resorting to "rigidities" of thinking he took an experimental attitude, adopting new policies with enthusiasm and abandoning them almost as fast when they seemed to fail.

Eisenhower, too, at the time of the Hungarian uprising in the fall of l956 was able to look at a map, see that a U.S. military intervention in the matter was unfeasible and politically dangerous, and opt for a non-interventionist policy that would minimize the domestic political repercussions in a party that had been committed to rolling back the Soviet Union in Eastern Europe. Quietly taking the issue off the United States National Security Council agenda at the height of the crisis, he allowed the issue to remain in the United Nations Security Council for several days, though nothing could be done there because of the Soviet veto. Only after the Soviet intervention in Hungary made calls for a U.S. military response unlikely, was the matter rushed to the General Assembly. These actions minimized bureaucratic pressures both in Washington and at the United Nations in New York to act in ways that Eisenhower would have to publicly oppose (Kitts and Glad, in press).

Sometimes, a leader may learn from past mistakes and avoid the kind of tunnel vision so often manifest in crisis situations. John Kennedy's behavior in the final phases of the Cuban missile crisis provides evidence of this kind of learning. Prominent in Kennedy's early formation had been the influence of a competitive, demanding father who had continually urged his sons to incessant activity and favored Kennedy's older brother in the competition among them (Kearns Goodwin 1987: 310-314). In the preparations for the Bay of Pigs invasion as Barber writes, Kennedy showed some of that old rivalry, manifesting "an almost personal animosity toward Castro" (Barber 1985: 281-285). In planning the ill-fated attack, this newly incumbent president allowed himself to be persuaded by an almost unanimous group of military and intelligence advisers of the feasibility of the strategy and the high probability of its success.

In later months, as relations with the Soviet Union worsened, Kennedy saw himself in a personalized contest with the Russian leader who, he believed, was bent on testing his mettle. Preparing for his first meeting with Khrushchev by studying all his "speeches, his background, even his psyche," he thought after the encounter that he had perceived the Russian's "'internal rage.'" Subsequently Kennedy characterized his opponent in terms that seemed to transfer to him the same intentions that he had himself experienced at the hands of his father. As the two antagonists faced each other down over a shipment of Russian missiles to Cuba, Kennedy declared of Khrushchev, "'That son of a bitch won't pay any attention to words. He has to see you move'" (Barber 1985: 281-285). Lebow, too, summarizes: "The President's 'gut' reaction was to treat the missiles as a personal challenge;" according to the report of one who was present, "a furious Kennedy exclaimed: 'He can't do that to *me*'" (Lebow 1981: 10-11).

Still, in the final phases of the Cuban crisis, Kennedy transcended some of these earlier patterns. Learning from his failure in the Bay of Pigs venture, he put less confidence in the consensus of supposed experts. The fact that much more was at stake in the missile crisis is enough to account for Kennedy's greater effort at consultation in the deliberation over strategy (Barber 1985: 281). Yet the propensity to learn from experience and modify behavior accordingly is certainly partly a function of personality, and invites comparisons with leaders who tend to repeat the same patterns of responses even when they have proved inappropriate.

Indeed, the peaceful outcome of the missile crisis, as Glad (2000) suggests, indicates that Kennedy was able to transcend, on this crucial occasion, earlier ego-defensive proclivities (Greenstein 1969: 50f). At the significant October 27 EXCOMM Committee meeting, for example, Kennedy was alone among his advisors in putting himself in the other's "shoes," acting on the basis of "empathy for the adversary." Suppressing whatever fears he may have had about manifesting passivity he also consented to a secret agreement with the Russians to remove American missiles from Turkey, a concession that enabled the Russian leader to back down, arguing perhaps that this concession had made his missile venture profitable.

3.5.5 Adaptation to the Environment

The leader's response to the more structured aspects of the environment in which he works calls for further inquiry. The relative neglect of this kind of work is due to two facts. At one extreme, institutionalists have declared that structures alone determine leadership behavior and that the study of individual choices leads only to idiosyncratic speculations. At the other extreme, some psychologically-oriented political scientists have viewed the environment as something primarily "in the eye of the beholder."

We suggest that these are false choices. One must consider the leader in terms of the choices he makes within a milieu that provides opportunities for, as well as limits upon, action. The actor is linked to the arena of action by his perception of it, but there are real constraints on his actions in terms of how others see the environment as well as the resources and barriers he must face in trying to implement policies. Yet the environment usually offers a menu of possible choices, not one narrow channel that must be followed.

As George Breslauer has noted in his recent study of Gorbachev and Yeltsin (Breslauer 2002), even leaders in the Soviet Union had some options. While sharing a common commitment to the "leading role of the party" in the political system, regional party First Secretaries organized some of their behavior around divergent political goals. The Brezhnevists (for example Grishin in Moscow and Romanov in Leningrad) insisted on the continuity in policy, accepting the corruption of the era. The "Puritans" (Ligachev in Tomsk), despising the corruption and fighting against it within their provinces, concentrated on rational, scientific expertise and orderly procedure to solve problems within their domains. And a few others, the "Reformists," (Shevardnadze of Georgia), were more involved in finding ways to decentralize the command system and build up a more efficient and legitimate party-led system.

By the mid eighties the consensus within the Soviet elite that something had to be done to deal with the stasis in the system made it possible for Gorbachev to build a coalition for change relying on the Puritans, the Technocrats, and the Reformists. He had some options as to the particular paths he would take. Choosing an incrementalist approach, he relied on Glasnost as a means of changing the political cuture before moving on to the establishment of new market mechanisms and new thinking in foreign policy as a means of cutting back on expenditure for the armed forces. Eventually, the coalition upon which he started broke down between those who wanted simply to eliminate corruption and make the Soviet system more scientific, and those impatient to move forward toward more democratic forms and a market economy. With these developments, and the unintended consequences of some of his early reforms, forces were unleashed which he could no longer direct in the manner he desired. Yeltsin, playing the role of "smasher," complicated his task by criticizing all his efforts. With Yeltsin's accession to power, the last remains of the old Soviet system were swept aside. But the tasks of building new institutions that would serve the people were difficult and Yeltsin was not always up to that task. Still, both men were system changers and their personalities and values shaped what they did. One need only imagine Yeltsin in the role of General Secretary at the start of the revolution to see that their personalities made a difference.

While Breslauer does not explicitly tie the differing leadership characteristics of these two men to concepts of personality derived from depth psychology, he does suggest certain connections consistent with that perspective. Gorbachev's role as reformer, his optimism, for example is connected to his positive experiences in his family and his polity. Noting similar characteristics, Glad and Shiraev (1999a, 1999b) suggest that these are the characteristics of a person with considerable ego strength—a strength likely to be the consequence of positive nurturing and good relationships in the family of origin.

For the American presidency, Skowronek has suggested ways of bridging the analytical gap between the "idiosyncrasies of personality and circumstance." Each president, he maintains, operates in an environment in which he inherits certain legal and organizational factors, as well as a cluster of ideas and interest groups connected with a past and a future regime to which he must somehow relate (Skowronek 1986, Skowronek 1993). But his values, his political styles and decision making modus operandi will influence how he interprets and adapts to that milieu.

We see the complexity of these relationships in the decisions of Dwight D. Eisenhower and Lyndon B. Johnson relative to military intervention in Vietnam. Though the constitutional options and limitations each man faced did not differ greatly, other aspects of the milieu did vary. Eisenhower had succeeded a president of the opposite party who had lost much influence in the last years of his term by supporting an increasingly unpopular American intervention in Asia. Indeed, in the presidential campaign of 1952, Eisenhower had vowed that he would end the US involvement in Korea. Could he afford another commitment now? Johnson, by way of contrast, had to take into account the legacy of his assassinated predecessor, John F. Kennedy, who had committed the US to efforts to save Vietnam. Could Johnson do anything less that that? (see Steinberg 1996: 80-81).

Still, certain idiopathic characteristics of the two presidents also played identifiable parts in their final decisions. In making his decision not to enter militarily into Vietnam, Eisenhower related to his advisors in ways suggesting that he sought a wide variety of opinions as to what would be best for the US national interest. Johnson, on the other hand, manipulated the processes to secure an alternative that had the most political support within the administration. Later, as he became more mired in the war, he settled for a policy in which he could neither win nor accept a loss. He seems to have entertained rescue fantasies that rationalized his growing commitment. Even his decision in 1968 not to seek reelection did not mean that he had faced up to the consequences of his actions. His diplomatic efforts were designed to bring the North Vietnamese to the negotiating table and, ultimately, if that did not work, to provide justification for further escalation. Personally, it was a way of "temporarily de-escalating without a loss of self-esteem" (Kearns Goodwin 1976, Milburn and Christie 1990: 247).

These differences in reality testing, discussed by Burke and Greenstein, were related to deeper emotional differences between the two men. Both had lively tempers. But, perhaps particularly when offered the opportunity to avoid confrontation, Eisenhower could shrug off his outbursts and redirect his attention to the matters at hand. Johnson could not. Eisenhower had the ability to empathize with the adversaries; Johnson could not. Eisenhower encouraged his advisers to speak what was on their minds. Johnson preferred "yes men" (Burke and Greenstein et al. 1989: 266-68).

3.5.6 Conclusion

As Greenstein has suggested, political psychology should not be relegated to explaining only residual behavior that cannot be accounted for in situational terms (Greenstein 1987: xii). Our point of departure has been that personality is potentially relevant at every stage of political decision making. However, what kind of a difference it makes, how, and when, depends not only on the psyche of the person who acts, but also on his or her relationship to others and the context in which action takes place.

It is a sign of the achievements of psychopolitical inquiry that the time is probably past when the whole range of applications of personality theory to politics can be encompassed, even summarily, in one volume. As evidence on many aspects of the psychodynamics of leadership accumulates, opportunities grow for increasingly finely tuned research schemes. The future lies not only in further delineation of the implications of certain personality types for political decision making, but also in better understanding the impact of psychological relationships and responses to environmental stimuli.

Challenged by historians on one side and increasingly competent and well-educated professional journalists on the other (see Brady, et al. 2000), political scientists may demonstrate their relevance to an understanding of political processes by embracing the exploration of increasingly complex and differentiated relationships. Their expertise, for example, is particularly suited to examining the interface between the choices of the relevant political actors within a cultural and institutional milieu that offers them several alternatives while constraining some others. To be truly empirical this science must look at how people actually behave in a variety of situations, noting both the rational and the affective aspects of those choices. The goal is to develop theories that take account of events that are recurrent, as well as those that are contingent; of the laws of human behavior as well as the choices that can change the direction of a polity—or perhaps the entire global complex.

Ultimately, this kind of work may contribute to formulating normative problems in terms that make it possible to apply disciplined analysis. Max Weber once asked, "What kind of a man must one be if he is to be allowed to put his hand on the wheel of history?" Weber answered his own question by describing the personality characteristics of a desirable politician as one with "warm passion" for a cause outside of himself, a "cool sense of proportion," and a "feeling of responsibility" (Weber [1921] 1946: 115-118). If Weber's specifications still coincide with present-day norms for benign and responsible leadership, the available theories and methods of personality research, put in operational form, offer the most promising approach to each one of these elements.

4 The Many Faces of International Political Psychology

Peter Suedfeld and Ian Hansen

Writing about international political psychology poses two serious problems of definition, which in turn lead to an even more serious problem of coverage. One difficulty is the definition of "international" as it applies to the field. As we indicate below, there are several non-exclusive possibilities. Second, even the definition of "political psychology" is hard to pin down. It is a field at the intersection of several disciplines, primarily psychology and political science but with incursions into (or from) history, sociology, economics, anthropology, communications studies, psychoanalysis, literary studies, linguistics, and even biology. Many researchers and practitioners whose work fits comfortably within these very fuzzy boundaries do not identify themselves as engaged in political psychology. Instead, they may categorize themselves as social or personality psychologists, political scientists, psychiatrists, historians, and so on. In fact, although the phrase, "political psychology," was apparently first used as long ago as 1910 (by Gustave Le Bon, mentioned in Dávila et al., 1998), there are scholars in the major relevant disciplines who are not even aware of the existence of a separate political psychology.

Even researchers who knowingly study political psychology topics may prefer to be identified with a better-known, mainstream area such as social psychology or international relations, which have many established university departments and employment opportunities. Such researchers also face a dilemma when deciding where to publish or present their work: is it better to seek an outlet that may be more visible and have wider circulation, but relatively few of whose readers may be interested in the particular research, or one that is less well-known and less accessible, but most of whose readers would be interested? Should one publish in the *Journal of Personality and Social Psychology* or *International Studies Quarterly,* on the one hand, or *Political Psychology,* on the other? If a researcher chooses one of the first two, the chances that the article will be noticed by political psychologists (or reviewers of the political psychology literature) diminish.

This problem may be ameliorated as potential readers increasingly use the Web to search out articles and books by topic and keyword, rather than looking through hard-copy journals and book lists, so that publishing in a focused specialty journal will not be a handicap. But that amelioration will not rise to the level of a solution as long as publishing in some journals is more career-enhancing than publishing the same article in another journal (i.e., as long as one's research is judged by the status of the journal rather than by the quality of the work itself). So the question of how many journals one must search in order to identify all relevant articles remains a difficult one.

Thus, there are unusual difficulties when one tries to review or assess the field of political psychology in general. The problems are exacerbated because political psychologists:

a. Study a tremendous range of topics, based on a great variety of theories and using all of the methods of the humanities and social sciences (and some of the biological sciences), with substantial overlaps across the boundaries with cognate disciplines and subdisciplines;
b. Present their papers at international multidisciplinary conferences, whose titles and tables of contents may not even mention political psychology. These may be the regular meetings of organizations some, and sometimes all, of whose topics fit into the areas covered by political psychology but are not called that—the Society for the Psychological Study of Social Issues (SPSSI), the American Psychological Association's Division of Peace Psychology, Psycho-Social and Medical Research (PSAMRA), the International Association of Applied Psychology, the Interamerican Society of Psychology, and so on through the world. Others are more focused, single-issue meetings such as the conference on ethnopolitical warfare held in Londonderry in 2000 (Chirot & Seligman 2001).
c. Publish their work in the less specialized journals of their discipline. These are usually mainstream journals, such as the *Journal of Personality and Social Psychology,* the *Canadian Journal of Behavioural Science,* the *Journal of Conflict Resolution,* the *European Journal of Social Psychology,* and dozens of others. More specialized groups also sponsor relevant journals. For example, the groups mentioned in (b) publish political psychology articles in the *Journal of Social Issues, Peace and Conflict: The Journal of Peace Psychology, Integral Studies, Applied Psychology: An International Review,* and the *Revista Interamericana de Psicología,* respectively.
d. Cannot speak or read all of the languages in which relevant material is published (many psychologists, and many political psychologists, primarily read the English-language literature), so that reviews of international research in any field are almost certain to be incomplete.

Although in some countries researchers make the effort to publish in English and in major international or US journals, this is not the case everywhere (cf. Feldman 1990, on Japanese political psychologists). In addition to language problems, there may be publications in books and journals that are highly limited in advertising, circulation, and availability, and will remain unknown to the reviewer.

For all of these reasons, the decision as to what specific literatures should be included in a chapter such as this becomes quite difficult. Below, we present a picture of how we see present-day political psychology in an international context. We will not try to offer a review of research on particular substantive topics, but will rather describe the characteristics of the enterprise as an international effort.

4.1 Political Psychology as an Entity

One aspect of international political psychology is the extent to which the field has a formal existence around the world. By that criterion, political psychology is certainly an international enterprise. Although the weight of people, organizations, journals, and funds is concentrated in the United States—as is the case for psychology in general (Adair 2003)—it is by no means overwhelmingly so. As Table 4-1 indicates, about a third of the 2003 dues-paying membership of the International Society of Political Psychology (ISPP) lives and works outside the USA. Nor is this global involvement restricted to mere membership. For example, in 2003 eight of the twenty officers and members of the Governing Council were from countries other than the USA. The President-Elect was from Poland, and the nominees for President-Elect in the next election were from Russia and Venezuela. Thus, the leadership also reflects the world-wide outlook of the Society.

Although the ISPP (housed in the US) is the major international organization in the area, there are counterpart societies in France (with an electronic journal, *Les Cahiers de Psychologie Politique)* and Russia. The ISPP journal, *Political Psychology,* is the primary "dedicated" journal. Other journals dedicated to the field are *Psicología Política,* published in Valencia, and the *International Bulletin of Political Psychology,* available online.

Table 4-1. ISPP Membership in 2003, by Region.*

Region	Number of Members
Asia	26
Australia/New Zealand	13
Europe	141
North Africa/Middle East	24
North America (non-USA)	19
South Africa	1
South America	16
USA	411
West Africa	4
TOTAL	**655**

* Data provided by Dr. Dana Ward, Executive Director, ISPP

Sections or divisions of political psychology have been established within some multinational professional organizations, such as the International Association of Applied Psychology, as well as in some national societies (e.g., the American Political Science Association). Many other academic and professional organizations, particularly in political science and social psychology, cover the area in their conference programs and journals. For example, the 2004 conference of the Social Psychology Section of the British Psychological Society "will place a particular emphasis on the discipline's capability for addressing, understanding and dealing with social political issues in the 21st Century" (2004).

To encourage and facilitate international participation, the ISPP has an established policy of moving its annual conference from North America to Europe to "elsewhere" (usually Latin America or Asia) in a regular cycle. The conference presentations themselves are authored by participants from several dozen countries each year, although the USA generally dominates in terms of numbers and many nations are represented by only one participant (see Table 4-2). Accessibility has a strong effect, as can be seen by the larger numbers of presenters from locations closer to the conference site.

Table 4-2. International Participation in Conferences of the ISPP.*

Participants from:	Conf. Mexico 2001	Conf. Germany 2002	Conf. USA 2003	TOTAL
Argentina	4	0	0	4
Australia	1	7	0	8
Austria	8	4	18	30
Azerbaijan	0	1	0	1
Belgium	2	6	0	8
Brazil	12	0	1	13
Bulgaria	0	1	0	1
Canada	6	8	9	23
Chile	5	0	7	12
Colombia	8	0	0	8
Costa Rica	1	0	0	1
Cuba	3	0	1	4
Cyprus	2	1	2	5
Czech Rep.	0	1	0	1
Denmark	3	0	2	5
Ecuador	0	0	1	1
France	7	3	4	14
Germany	4	61	16	81
Greece	0	3	4	7
Hungary	7	5	0	12
Israel	15	49	16	80
Italy	0	5	5	10
Japan	1	3	2	6
Korea	0	1	0	1
Kosovo	3	0	0	3
Latvia	0	1	0	1
Mexico	131	2	3	136
Netherlands	5	4	5	14
New Zealand	0	6	5	11
Nicaragua	0	1	0	1
Nigeria	0	0	2	2
Norway	1	0	0	1
Peru	1	0	0	1

Participants from:	Conf. Mexico 2001	Conf. Germany 2002	Conf. USA 2003	TOTAL
Poland	2	6	3	11
Portugal	0	3	0	3
Romania	0	1	0	1
Russia	0	11	2	13
Serbia	0	1	1	2
Singapore	0	1	0	1
Slovakia	1	1	0	2
Slovenia	0	1	0	1
South Africa	9	9	9	27
Spain	6	1	0	7
Sweden	2	15	4	21
Switzerland	1	1	1	3
Taiwan	0	0	2	2
Turkey	2	1	0	3
Ukraine	13	12	0	25
United Arab	0	1	0	1
United Kingdom	20	42	35	97
United Nations	0	1	0	1
USA	158	192	219	569
Venezuela	7	1	1	9
West Bank/Gaza	4	0	0	4
TOTAL	455	474	380	1309

* The numbers indicate how many participants from each country were listed in the printed program. At most five participants may have been double-counted because of multiple appearances. The table does not incorporate last minute additions to and deletions from the program.

It is not only conferences that aspire to international involvement. The longstanding Summer Institute in Political Psychology, held annually at The Ohio State University, has recently been supplemented by a European counterpart held in Warsaw. At the postsecondary level, courses in political psychology are still not a routine component of the curriculum, but neither are they restricted to American colleges and universities. Their numbers, and the number of countries in which they are offered, are growing. Polish political psychology has been particularly visible, with a special issue of the (English-language) *Polish Psychological Bulletin* devoted to the field, and significant research activity.

In summary, then, it appears that formally established political psychology is a thoroughly international activity. People calling themselves political psychologists are found in many nations, and so are organizations and organizational segments defining themselves by the term. Journals, conferences, and university courses likewise exist outside the US psychological heartland. It must be admitted that the majority of all of the above are located in Western countries, or those that are largely Westernized as far as the social sciences go: besides the US, these hubs of political psychology include the other former British "old" colonies (Australia, Canada, New Zealand, South Africa), Britain itself, Europe, Israel, and Japan.

4.2 Political Psychological Research in "Other" Countries

Research activity and publications are distinct from the existence of formal organizations and methods of dissemination. Here, we shall look briefly at the research on political psychological topics in various countries. Strictly speaking, any study dealing with a topic related to political behavior outside one's own country may be considered "international." Given the relative concentration of self-identified political psychology in the United States of America, the word is often used to describe research that either takes place outside that nation or is conducted by non-US scientists.

Acknowledging the incomplete nature of the reviews, what do they indicate? The rubric, "Political psychology in...." has been a fairly popular one. A whole section of the second version of the political psychology handbook (Hermann 1986) was devoted to it, with successive chapters on the state of the field in Latin America, Western Europe, and Asia. Just to illustrate the difficulty of reviewing the area, the first of these listed 50 publications spread across 42 journals, in English, Spanish, and Portuguese, published in 16 countries (Montero 1986). Since then, there have been articles devoted to general analyses of political psychology in New Zealand (Lamare & Milburn 1990), Japan (Feldman 1990), the Philippines (Montiel & Chiongbian 1991), Latin America (Ardila 1996), France (Dorna 1998), and Canada (Nesbitt-Larking 2003), as well as more focused commentaries (e.g., Feldman 1997).

Books dealing with political psychological studies outside the USA have also contributed to the literature. Some of these focus on a particular country or region of the world: for example, Ofer Feldman's study of Japanese politicians (2000) and works on post-Soviet era political attitudes and movements in Eastern Europe (Held 1993), Israeli political perceptions and attitudes before and after the assassination of Prime Minister Rabin (Peri

2000), and a pioneering study dealing with the attitudes of white South Africans during the waning years of the apartheid regime (Brown 1968).

Other books focus on a particular topic, and discuss how it is studied and conceptualized in different countries or in the context of different international events. Among the topics treated in this way recently have been political leadership (Feldman & Valenty 2001), collective memory for political events (Pennebaker, Paez, & Rimé 1997), public political discourse (Feldman & De Landtsheer 1998), historical reasoning in deciding to use military force (Khong 1992, Macdonald 2000), using mass media to predict such decisions (Hunt 1997), and ethnopolitical conflict (Chirot & Seligman 2001).

These reviews paint interesting portraits of the central interests and approaches of researchers. Topics of major interest vary from place to place, although in most countries there is lively theorizing and research about war and peace, political and social identity, socialization, intergroup relations (including those related to ethnicity, gender, and socioeconomic class), political ideologies and attitudes, democracy and human rights, conflict resolution, voting patterns, and political leadership. Another topic of interest is the issue of cultural differences, such as those between individualistic and collectivist cultures (Triandis 1995).

Some researchers have unfortunately interpreted this particular dimension as a simplistic dichotomy, a view that has been criticized within cross-cultural psychology on both methodological and theoretical grounds (Miller 2002, Schwartz 1990). Similarly, other cultural stereotypes, such as the supposed aversion of people from some Asian cultures to open disagreement—a generalization with obvious implications for political psychology—are also being modified in favor of more nuanced approaches based on current research (e.g., Tjosvold & Sun 2003).

4.3 Theoretical Diversity

In terms of its theoretical orientation, political psychology, even in the United States, is more open to psychodynamic formulations than are most other areas of psychology (a mostly disconnected area, psychohistory, is fully dedicated to these), and depth psychology concepts are very prominent in European and Latin American writings. Otherwise, the major epistemological trends of social science are all represented, from evolutionary theories through behaviorism and cognitive systems to postmodernist and constructionist explanations. Although cognitive approaches still dominate North

American psychology, they are not quite so prominent in political psychology; and the field is probably more open-minded about post-modernism than other areas of psychological research.

4.4 International Politics as the Focus of Research

We may think of international political psychology as referring to research or application that looks at more than one country: for example, comparative studies of some psychopolitical variable, or studies of the functioning of supragovernmental or regional organizations such as the United Nations, the European Union, or NATO (e.g., the recent study of UN and EU chief executives by Kille & Scully 2003). From this perspective, a major proportion of political psychology is international. Many of the classics of the field deal with international politics, written for the most part by people who were eminent political scientists or social psychologists before the term "political psychology" gained currency. The books of Lasswell, Jervis, Osgood, and Janis, among others, laid the groundwork for this set of concerns.

Although there are some works that at first glance seem to have an international perspective but are actually more limited in scope (e.g., Lehman 1993), much of the research on war and peace issues, conflict resolution, leader personality, sociopolitical identity, ideology, political rhetoric, mass movements, the media, and so on, routinely looks at how these topics are manifested across national boundaries. Recent issues of *Political Psychology,* for example, included comparative studies of farmers' protest movements in Spain and the Netherlands (Klandermans et al. 2002); nationalistic attitudes in several countries of the former Soviet bloc (Weiss 2003); Israeli and Arab perceptions of terrorism (Shamir & Shikaki 2002) and peace negotiations (Mishal & Morag 2002); and the cognitive styles and political ideologies of Flamands and Poles (Kossowska & Van Hiel 2003). A recent issue of *Psicología Política* is a collection of articles about reactions to the terrorist attacks of Sept. 11, 2001; although most of the papers study American attitudes, there are analyses of the communications of leaders across Western and Middle Eastern countries, a survey of public attitudes in Germany, and poll data from Canada, Great Britain, Spain, and Italy, as well as the USA (Stone 2003).

The cross-national nature of the political psychology research enterprise is further demonstrated by collaborations that involve colleagues from different countries. As one example, Table 4-3 presents the numbers of such collaborations in sessions at the last three conferences of the ISPP.

Table 4-3. International Collaborations on ISPP Conference Presentations.*

Conference	Papers
Cuernavaca, Mexico, 2001	11
Berlin, Germany, 2002	35
Boston, MA, United States, 2003	22

* The numbers indicate how many presentations (of all categories: individual papers, symposia, posters, etc.) listed joint authors from more than one country.

4.5 Internationalization: The End Stage of a Process?

Although in preparing this chapter we were somewhat dismayed by the multiplicity of competing and overlapping definitions, it is not our intention to choose, or even suggest, a "correct" one. That would most likely be a futile exercise, as there seems to be no *a priori* criterion for making such a choice (and in any case, colleagues would continue to use whatever definition they prefer). Nor will we attempt a round-up of the topics that have interested political psychologists in different countries, or of the research that they have been conducting. Rather, we want to bring into the field a more orderly and theoretical foundation.

We suggest that political psychologists take a close look at John Adair's discussion of the cross-boundary spread of psychology (e.g., Adair 2003; Adair, Puhan, & Vohra 1993). Adair argues that there can be empirical markers of the degree to which a discipline is internationalized, and stages that a discipline goes through in the process of internationalization. He suggests that the process goes through the following stages:

1. Importation: Psychological theory and research comes to be known in the country, primarily through the spread of journals, books, and speakers from nations where the discipline is well-rooted, accepted, and vital. In most cases, this means the availability of information from the United States and other Western nations.
2. Implantation: Native psychologists, following Western theories and methodology, produce work that is of sufficient general relevance and quality to be published in the major (e.g., APA) journals and by major scientific publishers, or presented at major Western or world-wide conferences.

3. Indigenization: Imported concepts and methods of psychology are modified to fit the local culture, with cross-cultural comparisons that demonstrate that certain Western concepts, methods, or conclusions are inappropriate or nonfunctional in the country. Note that this is different from a totally different "endogenous" psychology that is developed *ab novo* based on local traditions and worldviews.
4. Autochthonization: The local discipline base of psychology attains sufficient strength and respect that it can set its own priorities, develop culturally appropriate theories and methods, and make contributions to the science and application of knowledge within the country.
5. Internationalization: Interacting with feedback from the world-wide discipline of psychology, local psychologists make contributions that influence theories and research in the broader psychological community.

Adair identifies two major sources of the thrust from importation and implantation to indigenization and toward internationalization. One is the body of psychological theory and research that has identified limits to the generalization of "laws" from monocultural studies and has mustered arguments against total reliance on experimental methodology and positivist epistemology. The other is the need of developing countries to solve a host of social problems, a process in which imported psychology is seen to have only limited (if any) utility. As Adair et al. put it, "Culturally inappropriate social science disciplines distort interpretations of behaviour, divert attention from key social variables, and result in research that does not match national social priorities" (1993: 150).

We suggest that there are two stages that precede even importation. The first we call interest. This stage is characterized by Western political psychologists doing research on matters pertaining to another country, but only at a distance. This research may address a variety of issues, such as voting patterns or intergroup conflict in the country. The most salient example, though, is what is explicitly called "assessment at a distance." This body of research consists of the analysis of speeches and writings of political leaders and other decision-makers in order to draw conclusions about their personality, plans, decision-making styles, and possible reactions to various events (e.g., Hermann 1987, Post 2003). Aside from general scientific interest, such analyses may be performed in the context of international relations, when understanding and predicting the behavior of a foreign leader may be important for one's own country or for the world.

The second additional stage might be called exportation: the period when researchers from one or more other countries conduct research or apply their research-derived knowledge in a nation whose own social science community is either too small or not concerned with that particular discipline. Thus, political psychologists from areas where the field is well advanced may undertake projects in countries where it does not exist.

Adair (personal communication, 2003) feels that some critics may derogate this stage as exploitation or colonialism. We take a less dismissive attitude: the exporting of political psychology can generate and transmit knowledge that is highly beneficial to both its direct recipients and the wider human community, assuming that it is conducted ethically and with sensitivity to the cultural *milieu* under investigation.

For example, Ervin Staub, one of the most eminent political psychologists whose work for decades has focused on genocide and persecution, has for the past few years pursued a program of research and education in Rwanda, dealing with post-conflict reconciliation, conflict resolution, trauma alleviation, and intergroup peace. The project had no indigenous counterpart when it began, and it has systematically drawn in Rwandan students and professionals. This instance of international political psychology fits our definition of exportation. Ideally, its benefits will accrue to ordinary Rwandans, the social and health science disciplines in that country, and Rwandan society as a whole. In addition, science and practice everywhere will progress as Staub's team derives and publishes new knowledge from its experiences (Staub 2003).

We strongly disagree with any attempt to vilify such projects as inherently exploitative. Although not all exportation projects may be so benevolent, we consider the word value-free; negative terms should not be applied to all such projects willy-nilly. Much "exported" psychology—insofar as any research emanating from the West and carried out in a non-Western country is considered exported—may do as much or more to further development past the stage of implantation than psychology that grows purely from the local culture.

Let us consider where international political psychology stands in terms of Adair's taxonomy (plus our minor additions). First, we should point out that importation is a "silent" stage. Its hallmark is the consumption of Western political psychology, not production, which makes it impossible to assess from an analysis of publications, presentations, conferences, university courses, etc. Possibly a record of journal subscriptions, library books ordered, and visiting speakers might reflect how far importation has progressed, but such records are difficult to obtain. However, we can hypothesize that importation is a prerequisite for moving on to implantation and indigenization.

An analysis of the past 23 years of publications in *Political Psychology* indicates that, for the most part, international research is concentrated at the stages of exportation and implantation (see Table 4-4). There are also many studies with international content but outside the Adair taxonomy. These include cultural and cross-cultural research, articles that look at other cultures from a distance, and reviews that incorporate research from various nations.

Theoretical formulations and research methods are almost exclusively those developed by Western social science; although there are certainly large numbers of studies that look at local issues, events, individuals, and problems, these studies typically do not diverge from the characteristics typical of research from North America.

The reasons for this orthodoxy are obvious. Many of the scientists conducting the research received their training in the universities of the USA and other Western countries, and many of them conduct their research in collaboration with their former advisors or colleagues. Perhaps most importantly, even though *Political Psychology* is much more open than most journals to a variety of theories and methods (the latter emphatically including both qualitative and quantitative approaches); it too has its limits. Whether the journal's reviewers and editors would accept submitted manuscripts that seriously violate the accustomed criteria for such papers is questionable. As Table 4-5 shows, the data from journals that are not focused on the field, but that do publish relevant articles occasionally, are quite similar to those from *Political Psychology* itself.

Autochthonization and internationalization raise a related question. Do the "culturally appropriate" methods meet the criteria for rigor, controls, statistical analyses, replicability, etc., that are upheld by Western psychology and its gatekeepers? There is no problem if the work meets both Adair's definition of this stage and the normal criteria for refereed publication: i.e., if it is culturally appropriate and makes contributions to the science and application of knowledge within a country, *and* uses methods (e.g., personality scale construction, experimental design, statistics) that may be new but are in accordance with customary scientific norms.

Table 4-4: Political Psychology: Articles with International Content, 1980-2003.*

Country	Adair Categories					Other Categories			
	Imp	Ind	Aut	Int	Exp	Cult	CC	Rev	Inter
Australia	2	0	0	0	1	1	0	0	0
Austria	1	0	0	0	1	0	1	0	0
Bulgaria	1	0	0	0	0	0	0	0	0
Canada	0	0	0	0	0	1	0	0	1
Colombia	0	0	0	0	0	0	0	1	0
Denmark	0	0	0	0	0	0	1	0	0
England	0	0	0	0	1	0	1	0	0
France	1	0	0	0	0	0	0	0	0
Germany	9	0	0	0	1	0	3	0	1
Holland	1	0	0	0	0	0	1	0	0
Hong Kong	1	0	0	0	0	0	1	0	0
Ireland	0	0	0	0	0	0	0	0	0
Israel	20	0	2	0	3	0	4	0	0
Italy	1	0	0	0	0	0	0	0	1
Japan	2	1	0	0	0	0	0	0	0
Netherlands	5	0	0	0	1	0	1	0	0
New Zealand	0	0	0	0	0	0	0	1	0
Northern Ireland	1	0	0	0	0	0	1	0	0
Philippines	0	0	0	0	0	0	0	1	0
Poland	1	0	0	0	0	0	0	0	0
Sweden	1	0	0	0	0	0	0	0	0
Turkey	1	0	0	0	0	0	1	0	0
USA	1	0	1	0	22	18	20	0	19

Country	Imp	Ind	Aut	Int	Exp	Cult	CC	Rev	Inter
Australia & New Zealand	1	0	0	0	0	0	0	0	0
Israel & South Africa	1	0	0	1	0	0	0	0	0
Poland & Belgium	1	0	0	1	0	0	1	0	0
Spain & Holland	1	0	0	1	0	0	1	0	0
USA & Australia	0	0	0	0	0	1	0	0	0
USA & Israel	3	0	0	3	1	0	1	0	0
USA & Northern Ireland	1	0	0	1	0	0	0	0	0
USA & Norway	1	0	0	1	1	0	0	0	0
USA & Russia	1	0	0	1	0	0	0	0	0
Total	59	1	3	9	32	21	39	3	22

* Explanation:
- Country: Country of the institutional identification of the author(s). Thus, e.g., naturalized citizens or immigrants are counted in the country of resettlement.
- Categories:
  1. Adair categories:
     Imp – Implantation
     Ind – Indigenization
     Aut – Autochthonization
     Int – Internationalization
  2. Other categories:
     Exp – Exportation
     Cult – Cultural Psychology
     CC – Cross-cultural comparison
     Rev – Literature review covering international studies
     Inter – Interest, research on another culture "at a distance"

Note: Interrater reliability of category assignments was $r=0.95$.

Table 4-5: *Other Journals*: Articles with International Content, 1992-2003.*

Country	Adair Categories					Other Categories			
	Imp	Ind	Aut	Int	Exp	Cult	CC	Rev	Inter
Austria	1	0	0	0	0	0	0	0	1
Chile	1	0	0	0	0	0	0	0	0
England	1	0	0	0	0	0	0	0	0
Germany	3	0	0	0	0	0	0	0	0
Israel	2	0	0	0	0	0	1	0	0
Lebanon	1	1	0	0	0	0	0	0	0
Mexico	1	0	0	0	0	0	0	0	0
Netherlands	0	0	0	0	0	0	1	0	1
Northern Ireland	1	0	0	0	0	0	0	0	0
Norway	0	0	0	0	1	0	0	0	0
Philippines	2	1	1	0	0	0	0	0	0
South Africa	3	0	0	0	0	0	0	0	0
Sweden	1	0	0	0	1	0	0	0	0
USA	0	0	0	0	2	0	0	0	0
Israel & England	1	0	0	1	0	0	0	0	0
Total	**18**	**2**	**1**	**1**	**4**	**0**	**2**	**0**	**2**

* Explanation:
- Country: Country of the institutional identification of the author(s). Thus, e.g., naturalized citizens or immigrants are counted in the country of resettlement.
- Categories:
  1. Adair categories:
     Imp – Implantation
     Ind – Indigenization
     Aut – Autochthonization
     Int – Internationalization

2. Other categories:
    Exp – Exportation
    Cult – Cultural Psychology
    CC – Cross-cultural comparison
    Rev – Literature review covering international studies
    Inter – Interest, research on another culture "at a distance"
Note: Interrater reliability for category assignments was r=0.92.

To the extent that research fails to meet the first of these requirements, it is not autochthonous. Then, if it is sufficiently rigorous and significant, it may be accepted for publication in a major journal, and constitute implantation. On the other hand, some research may have serious and culturally appropriate implications for local (and even world) psychology, but depart significantly from Western norms in theorizing, methodology, or reporting. In that case, it may in fact have reached a level of autochthonization and *potential* internationalization; but it may not achieve that potential because it is unlikely to be accepted by a refereed "standard" journal, and therefore is unlikely to have an impact on international psychology.

Some may want to argue that liberation psychology, critical psychology, or other movements to empower the powerless and give voice to the voiceless fit the definition of indigenization or even autochthonization. However, they are based on Western theories—Marxist, neo-Marxist, post-colonialist, etc.—and use Western methods, usually some form of qualitative research. Thus, while some philosophers of psychology may perceive them as different from the mainstream (and they certainly are different from the mainstream of experimental, if not political, psychology), they are nevertheless streams from the same abundant intellectual seas.

One political psychology that seems to be truly indigenized, and perhaps to some extent autochthonized, is that of Japan. Feldman (1990) describes studies comparing "the Japanese case" with research conducted elsewhere. Topics include those prominent in political psychology everywhere: voting behavior, political socialization and leadership, and the mass media. Surveys appear to be a major procedural preference. So far, the level is that of implantation. However, some Japanese political psychologists, while replicating the methodology of Western investigators, emphasize the differences between their findings and those obtained in the original Western studies, showing the limitations of the latter and the inappropriateness of assuming that they generalize to the Japanese context –i.e., indigenization.

There is also a degree of autochthonization. Unlike social scientists in most countries, Japanese researchers publish primarily in Japanese-language journals. Among many, there appears to be a consensus that Japanese culture is so unique, and so powerful in guiding personality development and behavior, that findings from other cultures do not apply to Japan; and vice versa, that the Japanese react differently from members of other cultures to various situations and events. Among the unique features that Japanese cultural theorists identify are the primacy of vertical hierarchies in all relationships, the primacy of the group's common interests over the individual's, a need for intimacy with and dependence on superiors, and the overwhelming importance of social harmony. These characteristics have political implications that are more fully spelled out in Feldman's book on Japanese legislators (2000). Because these characteristics are seen as unique to Japan, they are also seen as unexportable; thus, the Japanese branch of political psychology eschews the possibility of reaching the stage of internationalization.

The case of Japanese political psychology leads us to consider Adair's stage theory more closely. It seems that different stages can co-exist in a country, which raises other questions. Does the discipline have to go through each earlier stage before reaching the next higher one, or is it possible to go, say, directly from importation to indigenization without going through the implantation stage? Is there any way to predict whether in any particular country the discipline will fixate at a particular stage, or how long the movement across stages will take? Is it possible for a country's political psychology to be endogenized—i.e., completely isolated from theories and methods that characterize the field elsewhere, and in effect isolated? And, what examples of internationalization (by Adair's definition) can we find in political psychology?

4.6 Lessons from (and for) Cultural Psychology

Perhaps the major candidates for internationalization in political psychology are to be found not within the literature of political psychology, but rather in cultural psychology. Broadly, the term refers to a research program encompassing work in psychology and anthropology that keeps awareness of cultural processes and cultural differences at the center of investigations into mental and behavioral phenomena. In cultural psychology, research and researchers drawn from the specific cultural contexts of many psychologically "underrepresented" nations are having a strong impact on the wider world of psychology. In cultural psychology, this aim is approached not by conforming to general psychology's assumptions and conventions, but by attempting to illustrate their epistemic limits.

Cultural psychology draws attention to the importance of cultural differences in some psychological phenomena that had sometimes been accepted as exemplifying "basic human nature." Politics is without doubt a cultural affair, and the findings of cultural psychology can provide rich sources of hypotheses and guiding theories for international political psychology.

The potential cross-fertilization between international political psychology and cultural psychology is related to many researchable questions. Perhaps one of the more stunning illustrations of how cultural differences can revise political psychological orthodoxies was the unmistakable verification of left-wing authoritarianism in the former Soviet Union (McFarland, Ageyev, & Abalakina-Paap 1992)—with the use of Altemeyer's (1988) Right Wing Authoritarianism scale (RWA). McFarland et al. (1992) replaced reverent affirmations of Christian religion in Altemeyer's original scale with reverent affirmations of Marxism-Leninism, generally acknowledged to be a left-wing ideology. McFarland et al.'s (1992) revised RWA scale predicted nostalgia for the old Communist leadership, support for distributive equality, opposition to *laissez-faire* individualism, and several other attitudes that the RWA scale predicts quite differently in North American contexts, as well as some things it generally predicts in all contexts, such as indifference to human rights and contempt for democracy (Altemeyer 1996). These findings have important implications for cultural psychology's concern with the context of psychological theories and data, as well as for political psychology's use of the RWA and the conclusion of some political psychologists that left-wing authoritarianism does not exist (Stone 1980).

While cultural psychology has not focused specifically on introducing autochthonous concepts and methods to the world, cultural psychologists certainly take these concepts and methods more seriously than most psychologists, and political psychologists may wish to do so as well. Consider a concept such as "face." Face is defined by Ho as "the respectability and/or deference which a person can claim for himself from others" (1976: 883). Psychological research on face is modest and receives little attention, and the most comprehensive research (e.g., Chang & Holt 1994) often concentrates primarily on relationships that do not rise to the level of politics. However, concepts such as face have obvious implications for negotiation and conflict resolution, which play a salient role in international political psychology.

Cultural psychology capitalizes most successfully on Adair's stage of indigenization. Cultural psychology has offered many demonstrations that reliable patterns previously established in Western research, and thought to be universal, are not always found when the research is replicated in different cultures or subcultures. Some of cultural psychology's findings are quite provocative and have stirred some controversy about whether key findings in psychology (political or otherwise) can be considered universal in any meaningful way as regards scientific prediction and control. A few cultural psychologists have even claimed that it is futile to search for some pan-human "central processing unit" beneath the noise of cultural differences (Shweder 1991).

A more moderate approach gaining currency in cultural psychology is to investigate even-handedly how cultural-educational and psycho-genetic processes influence and constrain each other (Lehman, Chiu, & Schaller 2004).

This approach acknowledges that there are obvious psycho-genetic constraints that prevent cultural education from being all-determining. Just as research on creolization shows that children are inclined to spontaneously generate a coherent grammatical structure out of grammatically inconsistent input (e.g., Bickerton 1981, 1988; Senghas & Coppola, 2001), there will be some cultural ideas and practices that are bound to be doomed by universal cognitive-emotional constraints. Consider a belief such as: "There is One God. He is omnipotent. But he exists only on Wednesdays" (Boyer 2001: 52). A severe program of behaviorist conditioning engineered by the most totalitarian methods might be able to imprint this idea on the collective mind of some human population; but once the totalitarian structure collapsed, the inclination of that population to pass this belief on to its neighbors and children should be vanishingly small. Although many arguably absurd ideas and practices gain popularity with little coercive engineering, some—like grammatically incoherent language input, and the idea of a God who exists only on Wednesdays—arguably swim upstream in their attempt to take root in human consciousness.

Nevertheless, cultural-educational influence has a surprisingly free hand in setting its own constraints on how psycho-genetic programming will manifest itself in any population. Cultural psychologists have found meaningful cultural differences in some of the most basic psychological processes. There are, for example, surprising differences in self-concepts and cognition (see Nisbett, Peng, Choi, & Norenzayan 2001, for a review). The need for a consistent sense of self is not as fundamental in East Asia as in the United States (Campbell, Trapnell, Heine, Katz, Lavallee, & Lehman 1996). East Asians do not exhibit Western-style cognitive dissonance (Heine & Lehman 1997), are generally more prone to attribute behavior to the situation than to internal disposition (Norenzayan & Nisbett 2000), and are more likely than Americans to accept two seemingly contradictory propositions as plausible (Peng & Nisbett 1999).

Cultural differences are also found in emotional needs. Japanese neither manifest nor reflect concern about self-esteem as measured by mainstream psychological indices (Heine, Lehman, Markus, & Kitayama 1999). Moral intuitions are also variable: for Indians, interpersonal responsibilities may supercede justice obligations, whereas among Americans the opposite is true (Miller & Bersoff 1992).

Cultural differences even extend to perception. When presented with a picture of a wolf set against a desert or a forest background, Americans can easily recognize that it is the same wolf; this is not so easy for Japanese (Masuda & Nisbett 2001). When presented with an animated scene of one fish swimming alone in front of a group, East Asians are more likely to attribute the fish's behavior to external (group-related) factors, while Americans are more likely to attribute it to internal factors (Morris & Peng 1994).

One's culture, however, may not be psychologically represented only as a singular and uncomplicated worldview that applies in the same way to all domains. Hong, Morris, Chiu, & Benet-Martinez (2000) replicated Morris & Peng's (1994) study with Hong Kong Chinese. They found that when participants were primed with reminders of Chinese culture, they perceived the fish's behavior in an "Asian" way; priming with reminders of American culture led them to perceive the fish in an "American" way, thus illustrating a kind of dynamic frame-switching between cultural influences depending on salience.

Cultural differences are not only differences across continents, or even across national boundaries. Nisbett and Cohen (1996) argued that a regional "culture of honor" leads American Southerners to differ from the rest of the US on a number of honor-related dimensions, including the occurrence of arguments that culminate in homicides as well as stronger behavioral and even physiological responses to perceived insult. Haidt, Koller, and Dias (1993) found that there were major differences in moral intuition about bizarre sexual behavior (sex with dead chickens) between high and low SES people who were recruited only three blocks apart in Center City, Philadelphia.

Although these studies do not directly address topics in political psychology, many of them have clear implications for the field. The notion that psychogenetic and cultural-educational factors mutually constitute and constrain each other can certainly guide inquiry into why Communist hostility to private property and market exchange was able to sweep much of the world within a few decades, and why it has so little appeal—even in nominally Communist countries—a few decades later.

Is Communism an idea like "God exists only on Wednesdays," something that can be introduced and kept in human consciousness only with the help of extremely unusual circumstances and extensive totalitarian control? Or is Communism an idea that fits very well into the cognitive-emotional architecture of a portion of any population, but has little likelihood of spreading non-coercively to the rest? In contrast, is insatiable "rational economic man" capitalism, in spite of its supposed cultural origins in Protestantism (Weber 1952), an idea that can spread with minimal help from a centralized government authority? Is the spread of desire for profit more suited to human cognitive-emotional architecture, or is it propagated in part by a different type of coercion? Perhaps people might prefer to work only until they have enough funds, and then vacation with family and friends for at least six weeks a year. This desire may become problematic to realize because economic externalities, fostered by a minority of enthusiastic capitalists, have transformed this natural human preference into a liability for long-term survival.

Psycho-genetic constraints are not the only relevant cultural constraints, however. Perhaps there is a momentum to any established culture that limits its own capability for cultural change, even if there is nothing about that culture which makes it more "suitable for human processing" than any other culture. Jesper Sorensen's (2004) notion of an immunology of cultural systems speaks to this issue somewhat. Once a cultural way of life has been established for a generation or more, what kind of new cultural-educational process, if any, could hope to transform that culture? Inquiry into such questions certainly has implications for the transformation of politico-cultural structures in "nation-building" (i.e., rebuilding) and similar enterprises. With regard to the Chinese "liberation" (i.e., invasion) of Tibet, for example, the five decade-long self-described attempt to transform Tibet from a poverty-stricken theocracy into a Maoist paradise (early occupation) or market-Leninist paradise (later occupation) have both run up against the millennia-long momentum of Tibetan culture. The fruits of market Leninism in the region are still enjoyed primarily by the Chinese (Han) occupiers, and it requires a large influx of these occupiers to attain statistics that indicate some level of Tibetan "growth" according to a market Leninist conception of cultural value, i.e. growth in gross domestic product, the balance of exports over imports, median income, etc.

With regard to international political concerns such as the "clash of civilizations" (Huntington 1993), the historical occurrences of regime change and occupation (e.g., Tibet by China, Eastern Europe by the Soviet Union, Poland by Nazi Germany, Korea by imperial Japan, etc.) as well as attempts to build a "culture of peace" (Boulding 2000, Staub 2003) constitute an incentive to study how likely it is that purposeful attempts to shape political stateways (political and economic processes) will be effective in changing the folkways (cultural and attitudinal characteristics) of their targeted environments (Suedfeld 2000). Some political psychologists have already done work partially relevant to the relative plasticity of stateways vs. folkways. Moghaddam and Crystal (1997), in their studies of the changing status of women in Japan and Iran, found evidence that while changes in stateways took place rapidly, folkways change more slowly.

In addition to offering helpful frameworks for inquiry into stateways and folkways, cultural psychological findings have obvious implications for how to be more psychologically apt at managing international politics. Morris and Fu (2001) claim that the findings of Hong et al. (2000) and Peng and Nisbett (1999) can inspire some imaginative solutions to cross-cultural conflict resolution. The authors suggest that when holding, say, Sino-American talks,

American negotiators might gain some advantage by holding the talks in a traditional Chinese setting rather than an American one. Such a setting may incline the Chinese side to be more compromising.

Kimmel (1994) explicitly linked US government failure to be aware of cultural differences in concern for face, dispositional vs. situational attributions, and personal vs. impersonal communicative strategies to its failure to prevent Iraq from invading Kuwait in 1991. Mishal and Morag (2002) suggest that the failure to negotiate peace between Israelis and Palestinians depends substantially on cultural differences in organizational decision-making. According to this analysis, the Israeli government is more "hierarchical," with leaders who can force their side to abide by their negotiated decisions. Palestinians are more "networked," and rely more on trust than on enforced contractual obligations to keep their side on board. The urgency of these topics helps to underscore how international political psychology would benefit from more acquaintance with the theories and findings of cultural psychology. Indeed, some political psychologists are already paying attention (Fiske & Tetlock 1997, Pye 1997, Renshon & Duckitt 1997, Ross 1997).

Cultural psychology, although it occasionally pays attention to explicitly political concerns (ter Bogt, Meeus & Raaijmakers 2001, Morris & Fu 2001, Schwartz & Sagie 2000), could certainly stand to be more aware of and forthright about political aspects of its investigations. Moreover, cultural psychology could also benefit from some of the textual analysis techniques commonplace in political psychology (Smith 1992). Although culture affects many human behaviors, its effects appear to vary by historical period. In the present era, the consequences of cultural difference may be gradually overwhelmed by the consequences of world integration facilitated by economic growth as well as travel and communications technology. Doing cultural psychology experiments in an age of globalized cultural intersection will tell us only part of the story of culture's influence on psychology. Perhaps it is time for cultural psychologists to study the texts tracing the paths of cultural development. Political psychology demonstrates that these texts would be useful not only for positing explanations for empirical psychological data, but would themselves also be a source of rich and provocative findings.

4.7 Conclusion

Our overview indicates that political psychology is a flourishing enterprise on the international scene. Although there are not all that many political psychologists in the world, they can be found widely scattered around the globe; and although the USA has more of them than any other country, those in other countries are active, productive, and prominent. There are organizations, publication outlets, and meetings everywhere. Research is conducted in many countries, across national boundaries, and on multinational entities, sometimes by multinational teams. Students learn about the discipline in institutions and extracurricular sessions in North America and Europe, and to a lesser degree elsewhere.

On the other hand, the overwhelming majority of this research is based on Western models. Theories, topics, and methodology follow the patterns of North American and European social science almost completely, regardless of where the researcher lives or where the research is conducted. Many political psychologists either explicitly or implicitly assume the universality of their findings, although limitations on the basis of cultural and other differences are often recognized. There has been relatively little work based on concepts and procedures derived from other cultures, which is not surprising given the norms of scientific publication; it is more surprising that there has not been more interactive feedback between non-Western cultural traditions and the concerns of political psychologists. Perhaps there needs to be a critical mass of colleagues with a variety of world-views for such feedback and interaction to occur.

4.8 Author's Note

The support of the Social Sciences and Humanities Research Council of Canada through a grant to the first author is gratefully acknowledged. We also thank Ivana Svetik and Tara Weiszbeck for their help in the preparation of this chapter, Phyllis J. Johnson for her comments on an earlier draft, Adela Garzón for providing copies of *Psicología Política,* and Janusz Reykowski for information about political psychology in Poland.

A list of the articles and journals covered in Tables 4-4 and 4-5 can be obtained from either of the authors. Requests and other correspondence may be addressed to either author at the Department of Psychology, University of British Columbia, 2136 West Mall, Vancouver, BC, Canada V6T 1Z4. We can also be reached by e-mail at psuedfeld@psych.ubc.ca or ihansen@psych.ubc.ca.

5 Political Psychology and the Study of Foreign Policy Decision Making

Donald A. Sylvan and Brent Strathman

5.1 Introduction

Scholars of international relations who study foreign policy decision making (FPDM) have long been partners in the intellectual enterprise of political psychology. Working in a field (international relations) that tends to underplay the importance of individuals in favor of international systemic influences, and often devalues the overall impact of agency in contrast to structure, the work of these scholars has a clear intellectual affinity for the intellectual paths of others who study political psychology. For almost half a century, these scholars have noted the importance of focusing on political psychological dimensions of FPDM.

A critically important work by Snyder, Bruck, and Sapin (1962) first included political psychological factors in its framework of foreign policy. In the era of "grand theory" in which these authors wrote their very title justified "grandness," as *Foreign Policy Decision Making* was followed with an obligatory subtitle, *An Approach to the Study of International Politics*. Specifically, these bold authors introduced concepts such as perception to an audience composed of international politics scholars that studied international systems and military force. Presenting a "model" of the state as an actor, Snyder and his colleagues evaluated factors critical to understanding the actions of states in international relations, arguing that understanding would develop and be enhanced through a focus on the topic of decision making. They emphasized that the manner by which decision makers understood what was going on in the world was key to the ways in which they responded, and in turn, to much of what happened in international relations. Indeed, their model had at its center "Decision making process / Decision Makers" (1962). This radical entry to political psychology—radical because it dared to argue that raw measures of power and capability of nation-states were not the only important variables in international relations—was largely met with skepticism, and thus the study of political psychology in international politics failed to "take off." Other major theories continued to ignore decision making, and concentrated almost exclusively on state power conceptualized as military strength.

After more than a decade long hiatus, prominent works emerged building upon the basic framework introduced by Snyder, Bruck, and Sapin. Some prominent examples include: Steinbruner (1974) whose studies of decision making employed a cybernetic emphasis; Jervis (1976), whose classic study of perception may well be the primary work in political psychology and international relations on syllabi today; and Cottam (1977), who built on social psychology to introduce images to the study of foreign policy and international relations. Each went into more depth regarding particular aspects of the manifestation of political psychological factors in the political world. However, it was not until the last decade or so that the impact of ideas and decision making on foreign policy were seen as mainstream in some areas of international relations.

This chapter will not attempt to chronicle the history of all such influences and academic debates. Rather, our gaze will be confined to a group of modeling and experimental works that have reflected upon the manner by which elite decisions in foreign policy are influenced by cognition and representation. These works regularly cross-fertilize with studies in both psychology and cognitive science, and are clear intellectual brethren to many of the other endeavors in political psychology chronicled in this volume. In short, this chapter will discuss the evolution of FPDM by evaluating modeling and experimental works that have successfully applied concepts from political psychology to enhance understanding of elite decision making.

The early works on FPDM played the taxonomic role that is so important in the intellectual development of a field. They tried to carefully specify the variables—many of them psychological—that helped explain foreign policy decisions and outputs. What they left for future scholars was the task of determining particular combinations and circumstances within which those variables would combine to produce those outputs. A variety of approaches have undertaken that important effort. Accordingly, this chapter will also examine modeling and experimental approaches that empirically examine relationships between such variables and build theories that go beyond the taxonomies produced by earlier FPDM works.

5.2 Computational Approaches

If Snyder, Bruck, and Sapin can be appropriately characterized as setting forth the list of ingredients—that is, how psychological and other factors influenced foreign policy decisions and outputs—other computational models can be seen as attempts to combine those ingredients into a recipe that produced foreign policy choices and actions. To accomplish this, computational approaches to foreign policy decision making often attempted to capture reasoning on the part of a state or decision maker. The approaches were frequently explicitly cognitive in their assumptions, and expressed theories in a linguistically formal manner. In so doing, the computational approaches took on the challenge of the late Nobel Prize winner Herbert Simon (1985) when he urged his fellow political scientists to learn more from their interaction with psychology than from their crossfertilizations with economics—which had resulted in the elevation of the assumptions of rationality to what Simon saw as an unreasonably high status. It was in this same vein that Valerie Hudson would present a rationale for employing computational models which focused on individuals and advocated a research program designed "to offer explanations of international behavior in terms of the reasoning, inference, and language use of relevant humans—whether these be national leaders, foreign policy decision making groups, or even scholars of international relations themselves" (Hudson 1991a: 1).

Building on the cooking metaphor, successful computational modeling attempts provided recipes (i.e., models of how foreign policy is created) based upon a list of ingredients (i.e., framework) first presented by Snyder, Bruck, and Sapin. It is important that we understand exactly what these computational models of FPDM do—how they are created, how they incorporate the insights of psychology, and what they add. In this spirit the following section delineates three generalized categories of computational modeling: rule-based (or production systems) models, belief models, and hermeneutic models. While the lines separating these categories are necessarily 'fuzzy,' they are distinct in *what* they are modeling. The common tie between these particular FPDM models is their emphasis on human reasoning and decision making. These models take up relevant calls from Snyder, Bruck, and Sapin, and from Simon to seriously address issues of agency in international relations and foreign policy.

5.2.1 Rule-Based Models

The first generation of FPDM computational models is termed "rule-based." Some researchers still employ these models even though their application to FPDM dates back further than other varieties of computational models. Rule-based models drew from political science and psychology to create a computer architecture viewed as congruent with the way in which humans process information. This class of models expresses theories of foreign policy decision making as "rules": simple 'if-then' statements considered to be the basis of human cognition (see Pennington and Hastie 1986, 1987, and Sylvan, Ostrom, and Gannon 1994).[1] Rule-based and most other computational models are programmed in object oriented computer languages such as LISP and C++ simply because object oriented languages better capture the conceptual relationships between categories (rather than those statistical relationships manipulated so well by computer languages such as FORTRAN). Object oriented languages have been chosen by many scholars of political psychology because they support one particular understanding of human cognition—specifically that the classification function is a crucial ingredient of human information processing (see Chandrasekaran 1986).

As just one example of these models, Thorson and Sylvan (1982) report on a cognitively oriented rule-based model called "JFK/CUBA," providing details for its rule-based operation and demonstrating tests of the model. The authors, building upon transcripts of the Cuban Missile Crisis and expressing their own theory of how foreign policy decisions are reached, designed a computational model that captured Kennedy and ExCom's policy making process. Their purpose in studying the Cuban Missile Crisis was not merely to add to the voluminous literature on that important event, but to study a well documented instance of foreign policy decision making in an effort to advance theory and enhance understanding of the process by which such important decisions are made. They designed JFK/CUBA to satisfy two important criteria: process validity (capturing the complexities and realities of the decision making process) and descriptive adequacy (capturing outcome validity). Their results suggested that both Kennedy's beliefs/initial representations AND the time constraints of the crisis influenced the ranking of possible options. Importantly, the model integrated cognitive insights into a theory of foreign policy decision making—including the crucial nature of a contextual understanding of the decision maker's assessment of the "state of the world."

UNCLESAM, developed by Job and Johnson in 1991, provides another example of a rule-based computational model. This model expanded the application of rule-based models to foreign policy decision making by modeling a *history* of foreign policy. Their contribution to these models was that the knowledge base, a crucial and static variable in JFK/CUBA, changed over time. By assuming that the United States policy establishment can be modeled as a unitary actor with cognitive functions that are similar to decision

---

1 Some computational models seek to create expert systems, where the programs themselves are seen as helping to accomplish tasks or solve problems. The research presented in this chapter, however, tends to employ such models to express and at times test theories of foreign policy decision making.

makers, Job and Johnson demonstrated computational models "can, at a certain level of generality, accurately replicate a history of U.S. foreign policy outputs over a six year period" (Job & Johnson 1991: 1-2). In contrast to JFK/CUBA's reliance on individual actors and contextual "state of the world" assumptions, UNCLESAM proceeded by focusing on general rules of U.S. interaction with given countries and paid careful attention to how those rules described events generated by U.S. policy in Latin America. As such, it advanced a different view of human information processing—influenced more by principles themselves than by individual attention to the perceived state of the world.

The psychological sophistication of the rule-based model improved with the advent of JESSE (Japanese Energy Supply Security Expert) developed by Sylvan, Goel, and Chandrasekaran (1990). JESSE modeled Japanese energy and supply security decision making in a manner that, while rule-based, was hierarchical. Consistent with the principles of hierarchical modeling, instead of being constructed by positing a large series of "if-then" rules (all of which are assumed to be of roughly equal consequence), JESSE begins by positing a series of contexts, defined as circumstances under which certain rules will apply. For example, JESSE posits energy supply security decision making in Japan is a "sacrosanct domain," in which seemingly contradictory policies are tolerated in the hope that some will ultimately help solve dilemmas inherent to the Japanese economy and polity. Interestingly, the authors improved the external validity of the model by basing initial premises or assumptions of JESSE on both secondary sources and elite interviews. By including politically important decision contexts, hierarchical rule-based models can better capture the way in which humans actually process information.

JESSE represented a theory of Japanese supply security decision making by incorporating cognition in two central ways. The first is the theory of context and hierarchical information processing explained above. The reader should note that these assumptions about human reasoning and information processing contrast with the assumptions of rational choice or subjective expected utility models, in that they assume intentional inferencing (Thorson 1984) and the centrality of the decision maker's problem representation (Sylvan and Thorson 1992, Sylvan and Voss 1998). In other words, consistent with a political *psychological* approach, the starting point in the model is the way in which a decision maker represents or understands the situation which she or he confronts.

The second way in which JESSE incorporates cognition as a central feature is by employing a theory of generic information processing tasks (see Chandrasekaran 1986) as the basis of their model. The venue for generalizability is thus the information processing tasks assumed to have been employed by Japanese decision makers, e.g., the generic information processing tasks such as "classification" and "planning" that they engage in as they make decisions.

In this section, we have seen that rule-based FPDM computational models incorporate many of the information processing assumptions that are so common in psychology, and as a result are able to improve and inform theories of FPDM. To be fair, it is important to note that rule-based models tend to be labor intensive vehicles for expressing political psychological theories of foreign policy decision making. Many are not parsimonious and some of these models do not generalize easily. However, they contribute to our understanding of the political psychology of foreign policy decision making by generating theories that integrate both politics and cognition. Our next section will deal with another set of FPDM computational models that, while often rule-based, supplement rules with overtly semantic elements.

5.2.2 Belief Models

Duffy and Tucker pointed out that belief models "include a semantic network for representing declarative knowledge plus a set of productions for representing procedural knowledge" (1995: 8). Rather than concentrate on the decision maker as 'processor,' belief models exhibit their political psychological influence by including belief structures, counter-planning, and precedent logics as important determinants of decision making. Belief models assume that decision makers have a rich sense of history from which to draw and make inferences. Accordingly, these models differentiate process variables (i.e., 'if-then' statements) from beliefs or declarative knowledge. This step then takes belief models in the same direction as hierarchical rule-based models when they diverged from flat rule-based models by implementing an additional theoretical driver—in this case, 'beliefs'.[2] This added module allowed belief models to 'go beyond' the information given and suggest how decision makers supplement incoming information with beliefs retrieved from a complex web of background information.[3]

---

2   For comparison, Sylvan and Thorson used political context as the additional theoretical driver.

3   An example of a belief model can be found in Carbonell's POLITICS (1978). POLITICS builds on and updates Abelson's Goldwater machine (a belief based model using conservative ideology as a driver for policy choice (Abelson 1973, Abelson & Carroll 1965)) making use of computational theories of human cognition as set forth by Schank and Abelson (1977). Given an event focused upon political conflict *and* an ideology to use in interpreting the event, POLITICS uses these computational theories of human cognition and

The semantic element of Taber's POLI (1992) is in the form of policy argument or *debate*. Taber captured the tension between competing paradigms by concentrating on worldviews (defined as knowledge "at a level between the individual and the organization: the level of shared belief systems, or paradigms" (1992: 891)). Crucial to the operation is an inference engine that "uses declarative beliefs to interpret the event, procedural beliefs to reason forward from its interpretation to a set of possible policies for responding to the event, and then selects a subset of these policies for implementation" (893). The declarative and procedural beliefs posited in POLI constrain the set of policies that an actor could choose. Expressed beliefs are inferred by Taber's stated logic to be consistent or inconsistent with particular policies, and the model only chooses consistent policies. In that way, POLI is able to explain events (such as the policies surrounding the Korean War) arising from debate rather than strict information processing.

While belief models add to the richness of the integration of psychology and foreign policy, they still suffer setbacks. First, belief models are domain specific. Because the operation and output of belief models depend upon background knowledge or belief structure, it has trouble spanning domains. Second, these models take a knowledge base as given. This knowledge base, however, must be discovered through interviews and data analysis. In some situations, this may be difficult to do. Further, in the complex reality of political life, rarely do scholars assume that knowledge is static. Indeed, the very process of decision making—successes, failures, learning, etc.—suggests that knowledge constantly changes. Perhaps an approach that considers learning is better for those studying foreign policy decision making. However, such dynamic models are elusive and difficult to construct. Some of the models to be considered in the next section adopt a different approach in this quest to achieve the dynamic model.

"generates a full story representation, predicts possible future events, answers a variety of questions, makes comments about how the situation can affect the United States, and suggests possible courses of action to be taken by the United States" (Carbonell 1978: 27). One difference between POLITICS and rule-based models is the independence of the knowledge (or belief structures) from the reasoning process itself. This design allows Carbonell to construct a model that demonstrates the important effects of two distinct cognitive processes: the representation and retrieval of declarative knowledge, and the processing or weaving of that retrieved knowledge into a policy decision. As with most other models discussed in this chapter, the concepts are posited rather than measured.

5.2.3 Hermeneutic Models

The third variety of models we consider are designed to examine politics and psychology in a manner consistent with constructivist[4] theories of politics. Given the importance placed on constructivist approaches by many international relations scholars in recent years, this class of computational models in foreign policy decision making seems particularly relevant today. We used the term "hermeneutic model" to refer to the production and reproduction of social structures contained in the ideas, beliefs, and language of simulated actors. Hermeneutic models differ from both strict rule-based and belief models by stressing the time dependence[5] of procedural and descriptive knowledge. Rather than assuming knowledge as static, these models show that only through trying to understand—or at least theorize about—constructivist concerns (such as the evolution of societal norms or the reproduction of social roles), can scholars grasp the multitude of possibilities in foreign policy decision making research.

Banerjee (1986) exemplifies the hermeneutic approach. To understand the construction, deconstruction and stability of social structures, as they contribute to the evolution of societal norms, the author modeled Piagetian development theory concentrating on social action schemata:

> "Through the subject, the schema searches the flow of social interaction for its stimulus. When it finds that stimulus, it enacts its act through the agency of the subject and continues monitoring for the desired reactions. If the goal is achieved, the schema is reinforced and continues its cycle, otherwise it is degraded. When a set of social action schemata interacts with each other so that each is stimulated and reinforced by the acts of the others, they constitute a *reproducing social structure"* (Banerjee 1986: 225).

Importantly, hermeneutic modelers such as Banerjee examine this process of structuration and reproduction by computationally modeling the psychology of individual actors and their schemata. The application of Banerjee's model to dominant theories of social science demonstrates its importance; indeed, in a later work, Banerjee applies his formulation to the development of Cold War enmity between East and West. For the author, the self-reinforcing structure of the Cold War emerged from social action schemata that developed and reproduced a tense social order, influencing the decisions, feelings, discourse, and debate of the Cold War period. Interestingly, this interpretation

---

4   For an overview of constructivism in international politics, see Adler 1997, Hopf 1998.
5   While striving to improve on the issue of time-dependence, these models do not necessarily exceed other types of computational models on the issue of cultural generalizability.

implies that the subjects interact meaningfully: "each is what it is because the others are what they are" (Banerjee 1991: 32). In schemes such as these, scholars view great power politics as two actors invoking adversarial scripts consistent with their developed social circumstance. As such, Banerjee's model is built on the core notion of schemata held by foreign policy decision makers. The very nature of these schemata contributed to the escalation of intense, negative relationships between foreign policy decision makers during the Cold War. In this way, Banerjee illustrated how schemata in the minds of foreign policy elites reinforced and reproduced the Cold War.

Hudson (1991) provided a different approach to hermeneutic modeling. Where Banerjee relied upon social action schemata as a fulcrum underlying dyadic relationships, Hudson suggested that roles, as defined by social structure, provided the scripts.[6] In other words, where Banerjee concentrated on how appropriate scripts evolve over time through social interaction, Hudson demonstrated how these scripts emerge from national roles in a power drama and explained that "to understand and project nation-state behavior we must first know the script of the drama they are enacting" (Hudson 1991b: 194-195).

Some argue that the main shortcoming of hermeneutic models is that they do not directly address "real world" political concerns, but rather engage in academic discourse. Because these models do not take particular, defined bodies of knowledge or social structures as given, they do not attempt to explain the outcomes of specific decisions. While the strength of the approach lies in its intellectual freedom (i.e., it can be used in a number of different domains and epistemologies), its failings lie in its explanatory power. In the end, the approach is helpful primarily for those who seek to create a discourse focusing upon the possible interaction of political psychological and social forces. As a result, hermeneutic models aid those studying FPDM who want to improve the discourse between academics, but disappoint those who seek "policy relevance."

5.2.4   Computational Models: Final Thoughts

The above pages suggest that computational modeling has followed three methodological strategies: rule-based, belief, and hermeneutic. The distinctions between the three are necessarily related to their specific concentrations. Rule-based models concentrate on the process of cognition—how information is

---

6   A script here is manner of communication that is pre-ordained by the context within which the participant understands himself or herself to be participating. The ubiquitous "restaurant script," which we all follow in that particular context is an example. Here, Hudson argues that the social structure of the dyadic relationship will serve in the role of the restaurant.

retrieved, processed, and used in constructing foreign policy. Belief models differ by suggesting that scholars should differentiate between types of knowledge. As such, these models illustrate the impact of differing cognitive processes associated with the descriptive and procedural knowledge of its subjects. Finally, the hermeneutic approach argues that knowledge is affected by a constantly reaffirming social structure. Thus, hermeneutic approaches examine the ways in which knowledge and actors interact with relevant social structures.

While we believe this trichotomy captures the essential aspects and character of most computational models of foreign policy decision making, the classification is neither exhaustive nor exclusive. As a consequence, some notable attempts have been left out. In this last section, we examine several 'mixed approaches' that do not quite fit the ideal types above.

The work of Hastie (1988) is representative of particular modeling efforts that fit into this residual category, and is the first model we mention that was created by a social psychologist. While not explicitly related to foreign policy, Hastie's work had clear implications for FPDM models by offering insights into group decision making—a social dynamic often at the core of foreign policy decision making. Hastie modeled human memory in the context of interpersonal behavior, suggested a role for computer simulations in experimental psychology, and applied some of his work to the study of jury decision making.

A further attempt by computational linguists resulted in the construction of computer models to increase understanding of the vagaries and usage of language. RELATUS (Alker, Duffy, Hurwitz, and Mallery 1991, Mallery 1991), for example, connected scholarship on linguistics with a sentence parser to model verbal representations.[7] However, in the realm of foreign policy scholarship, these attempts fell short by not explicitly connecting the implications of their models with the realities and complexities of decision making. Although Hastie may demonstrate the limits of human memory, and Alker et al. may provide inroads to understanding the uses of political language, the abstract quality of the work prevented use and implementation by many in the field.

Some of the earliest computational models—predating the rule-based efforts discussed earlier—concentrated on the causal mechanisms of organizations as policy making entities. These models simulated organizations such as the United Nations (Alker and Christensen 1972), collective security organizations (Alker and Greenberg 1977), and even specific states such as

---

7 A parser is basically an automated sentence diagrammer. This type of computational parser is consistent with such sophisticated non-political computational, linguistics based parsers as those built at Tübingen University (Schroeder-Heister 1989, Byram and Fleming 1998).

China (Tanaka 1984), in order to highlight the connections within complex political systems. They unfold in a "flow-chart" form, without the larger number of paths afforded by a rule-based model. By using the organization as unit of analysis, these methods oversimplified the politics behind decision making, often depicting organizations as static and unchanging. These models were a reasonable first effort, before the more sophisticated models already discussed were created. Despite the fact that they represented important steps in the computational approach to decision making, the simplification of cognition as it affects foreign policy decision making limited their use. Interestingly, the categorization in CHINA—WATCHER of all states as friend or foe, included one of the first attempts at an updating mechanism —which, in this case, checked to see whether another state has changed its U.N. entrance vote between Taiwan and the P.R.C., and updated the state as friend or foe if there had been such a change (Tanaka 1984). While not sophisticated, this was an attempt to bring some aspects of the psychologically important concept of reasoning together with political decision making.

More recently, Taber's EVIN model (1998) focused on individuals within the broader organization, and by doing so, more effectively incorporated political psychology into the study of FPDM. This approach demonstrated how information inputs within an organization (oftentimes denoted as bottom-up or data-driven processing) interact with memory systems (top-down or concept-driven processing) to create individual representations. EVIN exhibits the interactive and reinforcing role of an individual's motivated reasoning, memory structures, and the broader organizational environment (assumed to be an informational input) on policy selection. In doing so, this mid-level theory of cognition goes beyond the three categories first presented by concentrating on connections between procedure, beliefs, and hermeneutic learning.

5.3 Experimental Approaches

The above section commented upon the breadth of scholarship concerned with computational modeling attempts that integrated psychology and politics into the study of foreign policy decision making. We argued that the greatest benefit of the approach is the ability to test decision making theories in a number of different contexts. The ability to apply theories of foreign policy to a variety of realms is, of course, a desirable feature. But the assumptions of these models did not emerge spontaneously from the minds of scholars. Rather, computational models (e.g., Hastie's models) relied upon experimental approaches as an empirical basis from which to construct the foundations of their computational models. Over time, the internally valid results from social science experiments added to the literature in important ways.

Experimentation has proven a fruitful path for empirically based theory generation at the intersection of international politics and psychology. While some international relations scholars doubt the applicability of the laboratory as an empirical base, these experiments can and have contributed to the development of the political psychology of foreign policy decision making. As is well known by the audience of political psychologists, experimental conditions allow theorists to efficiently and precisely control and manipulate environments in order to gauge the impact of important variables. By controlling the external, structural variables (i.e., the environment), scholars of cognition and foreign policy decision making can isolate specific cognitive processes. Experimentation can also achieve a level of realism absent from computational models; carefully constructed experiments can replicate political situations. When combined with controls, experiments can grant theorists powerful tools of theory building in their attempt to understand foreign policy decision making.

This section examines the contributions of experimental approaches to foreign policy decision making. Two broad categories of research can be discerned from the scholarship. One branch concentrates on examining the content of human psychology, the elements that make up the human mind. As such, this branch examines the impact of memory structures, images, and personality predispositions on decision outcomes. The second category, cognitive dynamics, examines how these elements are woven together and used in a decision process. Here, the focus is not on the population or class of cognitive elements within a specific mind, but rather on how the decision making process makes use of these elements to make a decision. The following sections suggest how scholars of decision making specializing in foreign policy, and those specializing in other decision making domains, have used the experimental method to provide a variety of insights to students of FPDM.

5.3.1 Cognitive Structures

Scholarship on cognitive structures focuses on the different cognitive elements that 'make up' an individual's world. Cognitive structures can take many different forms, from schemas, to elements of memory, to broader structures such as 'world views.' The goal of this line of research has been to create a taxonomy of differing types of cognitive structures, and to connect the presence of these structures with foreign policy decisions.

The examination of images and their role in FPDM is one such approach that has provided a rich literature. Beginning in the 1950's (cf. Boulding 1956, 1959), then elucidated and expanded by a number of scholars (cf. Holsti 1967, Cottam 1977, Silverstein 1989), this literature concentrates on the "mental construction or mental representation of another actor in the political world" (Herrmann and Fischerkeller 1995: 415). The focus upon the image of the *other* is one of the crucial contributions of this body of work, since FPDM is quite frequently dyadic. Importantly, experimental work expanded the research by explicitly testing the manner by which images are constructed and connected. Herrmann et al. (1997) is exemplary. These authors demonstrate that image construction arises from three perceptual dimensions (relative capability, threat/opportunity, and culture), and then connect these cognitive elements to policy choices. In their words, the experiments "(1) define the sub-components of each image, (2) spell out the relationship among the components as expected in schema theory, and (3) establish the relationship between these images, emotional and affective feelings, and policy choice" (422). The operation of images during the Cold War is one important application of Herrmann's theories. These particular experimental findings have been buttressed by works that found a connection between images of the other state and policy choices during the Gulf War (Herrmann and Fischerkeller 1995). A later study examined the construction of such images and in-group/ out-group biases (Alexander, Brewer, and Herrmann 1999). Overall and importantly, Hermann's experimental work demonstrated a clear connection between social affect and the construction of images.

5.3.2 Cognitive Processes

The other major strand of experimental research concentrates on the processes of cognition. Where research on cognitive structures attempted to understand those elements that compose a decision-maker's mind, research on processes focused on how elements interact and influence the policy decision. Reasoning styles, or the manner by which information is processed in an effort to reach decisions, is an important issue in this research. Experimentally, scholars have demonstrated the relative weight and impact of reasoning styles in jury decision-making (Pennington and Hastie 1986, Pennington and Hastie 1987) and in foreign policy simulations (Sylvan, Ostrom, and Gannon 1994).

This strand of research is in part a response to cognitive science research (e.g., Schank and Abelson 1977, Kolodner 1993) that postulated case-based reasoning as the most important way in which humans reason. Authors such as Pennington and Hastie as well as Sylvan, Ostrom, and Gannon (see above), viewed this assertion as empirically testable, and undertook experimental tests to gauge its validity. These researchers found that explanation-based reasoning was more common than case-based reasoning. But even more importantly, these experiments determined that different individuals displayed differing propensities to reason with case-based, explanation-based, or model-based reasoning. Although other FPDM work (Khong 1992, Neustadt and May 1986) emphasized the role of case based reasoning in FPDM, empirical tests indicated that their work did not tell the entire story. The key for FPDM scholars trying to understand how such decisions are made is to correctly identify which foreign policy decision makers would employ which reasoning approaches, and under which circumstances.

Cognition is also related to leadership style. Conventional wisdom and classic research have supported the notion of "groupthink" and its negative influences within small groups (e.g., Janis 1972), including the emergence of defective policies resulting from the unwitting impact of leader opinion, the creation of climates which privilege certain ways of thinking, and the limitation of policy considerations to a limited set of options. Adding to this literature, Randall Peterson's work on leadership style (1997) argued that cognizance of the pitfalls of group decision making can lead to improvement of decision making processes, specifically "leader attention to how decisions are made rather than the substance of the decision will lead their groups to increased leader support, greater group confidence, a higher quality group decision process, and ultimately better decisions" (1117).

Interestingly, the social group processes studied separately by Janis and Peterson have been found to apply to masses as well as to elites. The survey work of Herrmann, Tetlock, and Visser (1999) demonstrated that a broad swath of Americans combined dispositional with situational cues when thinking about appropriate foreign policy. In an application of the survey experiment design, the authors determined that "people adapt broad predispositions in relatively thoughtful ways to specific foreign policy problems" (1999: 553). Their work provided a theoretical challenge to the post-World War II Almond-Lippmann consensus that the public had but a paucity of information, unstable opinions, and little influence on foreign affairs (see Holsti 1992, 1996 for more on this topic), and indicated that FPDM scholars would do well to include a more thoughtful public in future theories.

5.4 Non-Experimental, Data Generation, and Observational Approaches

A third general approach to the study of foreign policy decision making has concentrated on the effort to capture both foreign policy inputs and outputs by generating data uniquely applicable to foreign policy decision making. Work in this third general category has moved away from computational simulations and laboratory experiments in its quest to discover decision making propensities, and instead seeks to find statistical trends in large-N datasets. The goal, however, remains the same: the discovery of connections between decision propensities and foreign policy variables.

5.4.1 Pattern-Matching with Events Data

The group of literature that deals with the inductive discovery of patterns in addressing foreign policy does not have, in contrast to most works discussed thus far, an overtly psychological base. These works argue that "events" trigger foreign policy reactions, while treating psychological mechanisms associated with events or reactions as exogenous. Briefly, pattern matching approaches have attempted to discover patterns in sequences of discrete political events, described by "data strings." Here, the discrete political events are represented by strings of numbers generated by a non-statistical classifier program (for more information, see Schrodt 1986). The crucial assumption for this approach is that foreign policy (and decision-making in general) contains patterns that may be induced from the analysis of past cases. Two types of information are required—the sequence of events, and conditions surrounding those events. After specifying these data requirements, a computer can be programmed to discover historical patterns (Schrodt 1991). The statistical methodology employed is sufficiently sophisticated to uncover quite nuanced patterns. Although psychological mechanisms are not posited, the results of these types of studies have contributed to a psychological debate as to whether it is simply "tit-for-tat" or more sophisticated psychological mechanisms that are most prevalent in FPDM (Schrodt and Gerner 1994).

While this work adds to the study of foreign policy (most importantly, it introduces a powerful and important tool in data collection and interpretation) it suffers from several problems. First, to implement the events data approach requires a thorough and expansive coding scheme that can identify and classify. Identification, classification, and explicit coding of actors and their specific communications are necessary conditions. However, it is precisely this failing that prevents the general use of events data techniques across regions of study, since each region requires its own dictionary, specific to actors and events.

Second, the approach is largely atheoretical, especially concerning the role of cognition. Rather, the method assumes patterns exist in the ways that foreign policies evolve over time. This may not be a tenable assumption. Further, it is conceivable to suggest that in *any* complex system, simple patterns do emerge (e.g., Kauffman 1995, Jervis 1997). It is possible these patterns emerge not from the interaction or intent of states and the few sub-state actors coded, but instead from mathematical complexities and structural constraints.

Finally, the crux of foreign policy decision making is the elucidation of the decision-making milieu. Without a theoretical explanation connecting these patterns to decision making, the approach remains inductive and unable to distinguish causes (either unit or system) from behavior. In response to these critiques, authors have argued that "tit-for-tat" (i.e., actors responding in kind to either provocation or positive moves from the other side) is a genuine foreign policy phenomenon, not a statistical artifact.

5.4.2 At-A-Distance Measures

In contrast to the statistical manipulations of event patterns, "at-a-distance" measures probe the psychology of individual decision makers by evaluating their verbal statements. Literature on operational codes provides an early example of this approach. First developed to examine the underlying political beliefs of the Politburo (Leites 1951), operational codes are snapshots that "attempt to isolate the most politically relevant aspects of an individual's cognitive map and conceptualize them so that they become a set of general beliefs about political life" (Walker 1977: 130). George (1969) simplified the operational code methodology by suggesting ten questions that, when answered through biographical research, can describe the complexity of individual belief systems. Later works built on this foundation turned to content analytic approaches to acquire data that would assist in determining operational codes for individual leaders. Using these data, scholars evaluated connections between beliefs and behavior for presidents such as Woodrow Wilson (Walker 1995), and advisors such as Henry Kissinger (Walker 1977). Other scholars working in this tradition have applied the framework to foreign policy conflicts (Walker, Schafer, and Young 1999). Some of those same scholars examined how operational codes can change over time (e.g., Walker and Schafer 2000, Marfleet 2000). In general, this research has helped to further inform scholars regarding the role of psychological constructs in FPDM.

Among those scholars studying the impact of political beliefs on behavior, Hermann's approach (1980, 1984) is illustrative. Hermann performed an examination of six personality characteristics and combined these to form two broad approaches to foreign policy (participatory and independent orientations) over 45 heads of state. Her work demonstrates that general dispositions held by leaders—termed "broad orientations," accounted for more foreign policy behavior than individual personality characteristics. Interestingly, Hermann found that individual personal characteristics are most influential among those leaders with little interest or training in foreign affairs (1980: 44).

While many analysts have used operational code and political beliefs to chart and map the cognitive landscape of individuals, some suggest that this approach is too static. In a word, operational codes may grant a snapshot of the individual mind, but they cannot specifically predict strategies or behaviors within political situations. As such, some scholars argue for a 'motivation' approach. Quickly defined, "Motivation focuses on the broad classes of people's goals and goal-directed actions" (Winter 1987: 197). Scholars such as Winter have found that motivations, considered separately and together, are related to political actions and outcomes (Winter 2002: 25-26). Studies have found that motivations or traits can be discovered using a content analysis of Thematic Apperception Test (TAT) responses *and* when culled from speeches and other verbal materials (Winter 1983). Using Winter's Motive Imagery in Running Text method, motivations may be identified and assessed "at-a-distance" for political figures not accessible to researchers. Once motivations are measured, behavior is predicted and evaluated according to scores along three dimensions: the drives for achievement, affiliation, and power. For example, Winter and his colleagues have found that presidential success has been associated with a match between presidential motivation and societal motivation (Winter 1987); that changes in motivational pattern over time are associated with changes in presidential campaigns (Winter 1998); and, that changes in motivations are associated with changes in foreign policy decisions (Winter, Hermann, Weintraub, and Walker 1991).

Another at-a-distance method of note was developed to measure levels of conceptual/integrative complexity. Suedfeld and Tetlock (1977) designed their conceptual/integrative complexity method to enable scoring along a continuum that corresponds to variations in the ability to hold and simultaneously process complex links between concepts. By examining speeches and statements surrounding five crises (two that ended in war, and three that ended in a peaceful resolution), the authors discovered a link between higher levels of integrative complexity and avoidance of war. Further studies of crises and international conflict confirmed this finding (e.g., Suedfeld, Tetlock, and Ramirez 1977, Tetlock 1979). Endurance of this link was called into question by some disconfirming results (Levi and Tetlock 1980); however, further work on the issue of conceptual complexity, reinforced the findings (Dille and Young 2000: 588). Aggressiveness has been found to be associated with lower levels of conceptual complexity demonstrating that a black and white, dichotomous, view of the world is related to the unwillingness or inability to find other solutions (e.g., Driver 1977). While initial work emphasized the stability of conceptual complexity as a personality trait or cognitive style (Hermann 1980), later work also identified the importance of situation or environment (Hermann and Hermann 1989), indicating that whether an individual leader processes information in a complex versus a simple manner will also be influenced by the relevant environment.

While there are obvious benefits to the method, some have critiqued the validity of at-a-distance methods by quarrelling with the selection of source material. Here, the debate has centered on the use of either spontaneous or prepared remarks. The conventional wisdom suggests that spontaneous remarks are more representative of a leader's psychological makeup, and are most appropriate for at-a-distance techniques (see Winter et al. 1991a). However, there are problems with using spontaneous material. For example, Dille and Young (2000) found that trait measurements taken from spontaneous remarks are less stable then those taken from prepared remarks. In addition, Dille (2000) found that prepared remarks may in fact be useful indicators if leaders were actively involved in crafting the prepared statement. The lesson for practitioners in this domain has been to exercise caution in the selection of appropriate data.

The use of these particular methods have also stimulated a further line of critique which questions theories of cognition underlying the method, and asks whether it is in fact, a method without a theory. While the above suggests the utility of the method in identifying certain predispositions, less is written about connecting cognitive theories to these predispositions. For example, while Hermann (1980) associates low levels of conceptual complexity scores with aggressive foreign policy, there are no theories of cognition discussed. This may not be a large issue—it is fair to say that seeing the world in a black and white fashion can lead to aggressiveness as a solution. However, only additional theoretical work can satisfactorily unpack the complex interaction of psychology and decision.

5.5 Political Psychology and Social Constructivism

Is there a complementarity between political psychology and (social) constructivism? In one regard the complementarity is clear: while constructivist approaches (e.g., Hopf 2002) seek to understand societal norms, aspects of political psychology can be seen to offer plausible understandings of how and why individuals help create such norms. It is not that simple, though. At times, practitioners of political psychology undervalue social factors including societal norms, while constructivists sometimes overtly eschew study of psychological factors. Hopf (2002) undertakes a constructivist study of Soviet and Russian politics which overtly draws on literature within psychology, as does Adler's (1997) argument about the intellectual basis of constructivism. We concur with Adler's assertion that one of the critical questions not presently satisfactorily addressed by international relations scholars is "how and why do certain collective expressions of human understanding, neither valid nor true, *a priori*, develop into social practices, become firmly established within social and political systems, spread around the world and become reified or taken for granted?" (1997: 337). Some might point to the Serbian understanding of massacres in Kosovo as an example. Adler and Hopf each point in the direction of cognitive bases for such collective expressions. The tasks of understanding such cognitive bases can and should be undertaken by scholars working in the political psychology tradition explicated in this chapter. While computational models such as JESSE (Sylvan, Chandrasekaran, and Goel 1990) and perhaps UNCLESAM (Job and Johnson 1991) take rudimentary steps in that direction, much work remains. An important challenge ahead for those who seek to systematically study the political psychology of foreign policy is to continue to develop theories and models that improve on these efforts to capture cognitive dimensions in the operation of foreign policy decision making.

5.6 Conclusions: Do We Understand More About FPDM Through The Lens of Political Psychology?—and—Where Do We Go From Here?

In a chapter that was added to the new edition of Snyder, Bruck, and Sapin's classic volume (2002), Hudson concludes that international relations scholars are now more closely examining the questions addressed by Snyder, Bruck, and Sapin (1962), and in so doing have produced methodological breakthroughs. Many of these breakthroughs, particularly those in computational modeling, have been highlighted in the work examined in this chapter. We concur with Hudson's assertion. Despite her observation and the fact that many of the categories of scholarship in this chapter are defined by the techniques employed, we now believe that paying less attention to the trappings of our research and more attention to the substance of knowledge necessary to better undertake Snyder, Bruck, and Sapin's original challenge—that is, to understand relationships between factors (many of them psychological) that produce foreign policy—is a key task of those studying political psychology and foreign policy decision making. Accordingly, we offer the following suggestions to build on the progress that has been outlined in this chapter:

1. With the help of such FPDM scholars as Taber (1992, 1998), and Sylvan, Goel, and Chandrasekaran (1990), we now understand that problem-solving heuristics employed by leaders are important to understanding the foreign policy decision making process. Therefore, we must more carefully examine those situations under which particular heuristics manifest themselves in foreign policy decision making. Specifically, by studying regularities in the invocation of particular heuristics by decision makers (i.e., circumstances under which the heuristic is most likely to be invoked), we can move toward a more complete—perhaps even algorithmic—theory of various types of foreign policy decision making.

2. There is presently a great deal of sophisticated computational linguistics research, often focusing on the creation of parsers (cf. Schroeder-Heister (1989), Byram and Fleming (1998)), underway in Europe. Exemplary agent based modeling work has also been accomplished by European scholars (cf. Cederman (1997)). A crucial task at this juncture would be to build bridges between these European research programs and those which have received focus in this chapter. The emphasis of many U.S. projects on the substance of politics, and in particular foreign policy decision making, may enhance the integration of political psychological factors into explanations of foreign policy and can cross-fertilize with some of the sophisticated methodologies employed in fields other than political science (such as linguistics) and primarily in Europe. The goal here would be to express theories of FPDM in a more malleable manner, ready for creative manipulation and testing.

3. We must enhance the dialogue between conclusions based upon laboratory experiments and arguments garnered from analysis of "real world" foreign policy situations. Many of the models discussed in this chapter could be substantially enriched with a stronger empirical basis. That empirical basis could be achieved in the laboratory and/or in the "real world." Each of these bases of observation offers an advantage. The

laboratory offers control, allowing the isolation of specific variables in order to assess their impact. The "real world," as represented by primary and secondary source accounts of foreign policy, provides more external validity than experimental analysis.

4. The study of FPDM in international relations witnesses battles between those who pose their questions and answers at a very grand level (e.g., "Which global forces lead to war?"), often assuming all decision making to be "rational," and those who study more micro-level questions, such as most of the decision making puzzles addressed in this chapter, often adopting the terminology of psychology, not assuming rationality of decision makers, and at times ignoring the "big picture." Dialogue (called for by Chollet and Goldgeier in the revised Snyder, Bruck, and Sapin 2002: 153-180) between these traditions is crucial to progress in the study of international relations. It is equally important not to create a contest where one tradition is deemed to be correct. We should reinforce the notion that rationality is not the issue by studying how decisions are made, rather than positing rationality or classifying work in terms of pro- or anti-rational choice. Perhaps the insights of Kahneman, Slovik, and Tversky; as well as those of Thorson; and the work of Sylvan and Voss (the latter two research projects were argued earlier in this chapter to underlie computational models such as JFK/CUBA and JESSE); can inform those whose starting point has been theories of rational choice. This could result in greater comprehension of FPDM processes.

5. Studying "speechmaking as policymaking" (Chollet and Goldgeier in Snyder, Bruck, and Sapin 2002) is important. Public representations are a significant part of politics. Building upon work on discourse analysis (Hopf), linguistics (Byram and Fleming 1998), and text analysis (Voss 1998), we need to apply the insights of political psychology to these fields to understand the roots and dynamics of such public representations. The FPDM traditions of computational parsers and hermeneutic models discussed in this chapter do view words as politics and/or speechmaking as policymaking. Continuing to build on these works and enhancing the sophistication of the political psychology underlying these endeavors has the potential to increase our understanding of FPDM and international relations.

This chapter has argued that the study of FPDM has taken on a distinct political psychological flavor in recent years. Perhaps the five suggestions above can continue to expand the influence of ideas from political psychology in an effort to better understand foreign policy decision making. What is being proposed here, unapologetically, is a research program in FPDM that is both enhanced by an expanded attention to political psychology, and integrated in significant ways with other, non-psychological, efforts in international relations. The time has come for FPDM scholars to stop feuding with those who have not yet understood the importance of political psychological approaches in international relations. It is also time for those studying FPDM to increase the sophistication of our own work while building bridges to other international relations traditions. Our entire scholarly community will then benefit with an enhanced understanding of foreign policy as a component of international relations.

6 Refocusing Political Psychology: The Search for a Twenty-First Century Agenda

David G. Winter

6.1 The Real-World Foundations of Political Psychology

The rise of political psychology in the middle decades of the twentieth century, like that of other interdisciplinary fields (see Klein 1996), can be understood as an intellectual response to the practical political problems and concerns of that era. For example, Harold Lasswell (1930, 1936, 1948), who was a major resource and inspiration to the first generation of political psychologists, tried to develop a psychological analysis and understanding of fascist and communist challenges to democratic political systems in the 1930s and 1940s. World War II created many problems for political scientists and psychologists: understanding the leadership process in general (in domestic and international politics, in combat) and the personalities of certain leaders (Hitler, Stalin) in particular; measuring and changing civilian and military attitudes and morale; and identifying collective psychological characteristics ("national character") of enemies, allies, and even one's own country. The approaches and technologies developed in the 1940s to solve these problems constituted much of the canon of the new field of political psychology.

As the Cold War emerged from the ashes of World War II, the American desire to "contain" the Communist bloc while avoiding another world war—as well as the desire of many to identify alternatives to aggression—focused intellectual energy and research funds on topics of deterrence, perceptions and misperceptions in international relations, crisis management, bargaining, conflict resolution, negotiation and compromise (see, for example, White 1986)—all of which have become staple topics within political psychology.

In the domestic U.S. political arena, meanwhile, political psychologists and political consultants adapted wartime survey research techniques to understand and measure how people perceive candidates and issues, why they vote, and why they vote as they do (see Converse 1987). As campaign efforts and budgets became more and more concentrated on television, political psychologists developed sophisticated measures of political cognition to explore the nature and extent of media effects on attitudes, opinions, and voting. In between elections, both incumbents and challengers studied public opinion polls in relation to government policies and choices, all in an effort to improve their chances at the next election (see Iyengar and McGuire 1993).

These efforts to understand and then influence the psychological bases of inter-state relations, and of the democratic process, thus gave a major impetus to theory, research, and education in political psychology.[1] And to be sure, the field has been well-served by these twentieth-century agendas. Political psychologists have developed sophisticated ways to measure psychological variables (traits, motives, cognitions, opinions, values, and so forth) both among individual world leaders and in the public at large. They have developed elaborate statistical models to understand the processes of opinion formation, voting, decision-making, conflict escalation and de-escalation, and negotiation. At the same time, they have begun to make contact with other late twentieth-century intellectual currents, such as gender studies and post-modernism. Along these lines, Winter (2000, 2002) argued that political psychology is uniquely poised to understand the terrible confluence of power, sex, and violence that characterized the twentieth century, and suggested that political psychology devote theoretical and empirical attention to three broad topics growing out of such a confluence: (1) understanding the striving for power, which (especially in the context of perceived "difference") often leads to violence; (2) understanding the construction of difference itself, with gender being perhaps the original prototype or template for all other constructed differences; and (3) exploring whether it is possible for people and societies to live "beyond" power and difference.

6.2 Globalization in the Twenty-First Century

The first decade of the twenty-first century is a good time to consider the future of political psychology. World War II is now more than sixty years in the past, and the Cold War is now a fading memory (hardly even that in the minds of our youngest students). What are the social challenges, problems, and opportunities that will dominate the first half of the twenty-first century? Will they require political psychologists to change or add to their intellectual framework in the decades to come?

---

1   This is especially true for the United States. Elsewhere, the defining role of these developments was supplemented by additional emphases: for example, a concern with broader social theory (especially Marxism) and the influence of political structures and events on psychological phenomena in Western Europe (Bryder 1986), power-dependency and collectivism in Asia (Pye 1986), and nationalism and social activism in Latin America (Montero 1986).

People who try to predict future trends, especially intellectual and scientific trends, often end up looking more foolish than prescient. Over the next hundred years, what will be the political and psychological impact of the growth of the world's population, or the ratio of population to resources (Kaplan, 1996)? What about climate change, some new lethal virus, or terrorism? Or should we be concerned about more subtle trends, such as the changing age structure of the population—as more and more people in more and more countries enter the "third age" (Laslett 1996) between retirement and disability-death? No one can know for sure.

However, I believe that even now we can see that many trends, issues, and problems of the next fifty years are related to the broad topic of globalism or globalization (see Gilpin 2000; Hardt & Negri 2000; Micklethwait & Wooldridge 2000, Soros 2002, and the proliferation of other books on this topic[2]). Globalization may subsume many of the other trends referred to above. Driven in the first instance by technology and capitalist organization, our world is becoming more and more connected and related. In economics, politics, cultural forms, consumer goods, and the mass media, structures that are transnational, transcultural, and "universal" are beginning to override local identities, local moralities, local relationships, and local political processes. Globalization itself has several specific components: (1) What is "produced" is often more abstract and less substantial than were the manufactured products of a hundred years ago. (2) Revolutions in communication have greatly increased the speed and extent of information transmission and thereby the diffusion of fashions, images, ideas, and culture. At the same time, there are downsides: (3) Sites of production have become more mobile, the product life-cycle from innovation to obsolescence is shorter and less predictable, and economic parameters (costs, prices, returns, and share prices) are more volatile. (4) The "imperatives of the market" force corporations to emphasize return on investment instead of employee loyalty and other intangible factors. (5) Control over a nation's economy, mass media, cultural institutions, laws and even customs has shifted from national governments toward various supranational governments and nongovernmental institutions.

Globalization is thereby likely to create new practical problems for the twenty-first century, as well as altering the terms of enduring problems such as war and elections. While the likelihood of inter-state wars between major powers may be reduced, governments are faced with increased intra-state,

---

2   In September 2003, for example, one major academic bookstore had a separate section on "globalization," with a total of 128 different titles.

non-state, "polystate," and terrorist violence. How will these affect the intellectual, methodological, and educational agendas of political psychology?

6.2.1 Attractions and Preconditions of Globalization

In many respects, globalization is highly attractive to many people and groups around the world, although it is important to realize that these benefits are not distributed evenly and universally. It brings new and better goods at lower prices, the possibility of greater material prosperity (or at least escape from poverty), and new culture—ideas, fashions, foods, and music. More abstractly, globalization offers a vastly expanded sense of possibility: that is, what one might be, do, and become (see, for example, Arnett 2002). It offers an expanded sense of self and social identity. Globalization means variety, complexity, excitement, arousal. In terms of opportunities for both real travel and also symbolic identity, people can now become "citizens of the world." For some, it may even offer the possibility of escaping one's personal problems.

For reasons such as these, some people have throughout history been drawn into wider, more cosmopolitan and "globalized" identities and ways of life. In the Roman Empire, for example, people from places and nations as diverse as Spain, Britain, Anatolia, and North Africa took pride in the claim, "Civis Romanus Sum" ("I am a Roman citizen"). St. Paul—a devout Jew who first persecuted and then propagated a new religion—appealed to Caesar when he was about to be flogged in Jerusalem, asking: "Can you legally flog a man who is a Roman citizen?" (Acts 25:11, 22:25).[3] In every multinational empire, there are always people drawn from the colonies to the metropole, like Michener's fictional character Andrzej Lubonski in his novel *Poland:* "As a Pole he missed the Vistula, and his castle, and his vast estates in Galicia, and the winter visits to Warsaw, but in Vienna ['the center of the world'] there were compensations . . . he played a major role in the governance of this city and the empire which it represented" (1983: 280, 277). And Hélène Jutras, at the time a young francophone law student, born and raised in the heartland of Quebec separatism, wrote a book entitled *Québec is Killing Me* (Jutras 1995), in which she argued that nationalism is suffocating, backward, and unfulfilling, in contrast to the sophistication, intellectual stimulation, and personal enhancement of a more cosmopolitan life.

---

3   In response: "Then those who were about to examine him withdrew hastily, and the commandant himself was alarmed when he realized that Paul was a Roman citizen and that he had put him in irons" (Acts 22:29).

These material and psychological attractions suggest certain broad cultural and psychological prerequisites for globalization to take root in countries, groups, and people: "stimulus-seeking" or the quest for novelty and complexity (Fiske & Maddi 1961), achievement motivation (McClelland 1961), the desire for prestige and power (Winter 1973), as well as the desire to escape tightly-constrained and limited identities (Winter, Stewart, Henderson-King, & Henderson-King 2001). Political psychologists are uniquely poised to understand these psycho-political preconditions—and therefore the successes and failures—of globalization.

6.2.2 Dangers and Risks of Globalization

Despite its attractions and promise, globalization also has many possible downsides: dangers, risks, and negative consequences. Because of their potential for disruptive and disastrous outcomes, the description, elucidation, and analysis of these negative effects is even more important for the twenty-first century agenda of political psychology. In the following sections, I suggest some of the negative aspects of globalization that have already become clear in recent experience, along with their individual and collective psychological-political consequences.[4]

6.2.3 Control, Legitimacy, and the Ironic Fate of Individualism

With globalization, decisions about the organization of production and distribution pass from managers and directors of freestanding local units to remote (even invisible) groups of strangers. Similarly, control and regulation of a nation-state's economic life—for example, regulation of inflation, interest rates, employment, and norms governing employment practices and the environment—are ceded to supranational bureaucracies and trans-national corporate boards and managers. As a result, both individual workers and political leaders experience a loss of traditional means of control—both directly, in the workplace, and indirectly, through the decreased importance of voting and political participation.

At one level, this loss of control constitutes a crisis of legitimacy for the bureaucracies of globalization. In the words of the protesters at the December 1999 Seattle meeting of the World Trade Organization, echoed by later similar

---

4 In an earlier discussion (Winter, 2003), I assessed the emotional effects of globalization under the headings of power and control, incompetence, uncertainty, and anger.

protests at other similar meetings: "Who elected you?" That is, bureaucracy cannot legitimize itself. As Max Weber argued, "at the top of every bureaucratic organization, there is necessarily an element which is at least not purely bureaucratic" ([1922]1968: 222).⁵ In the end, therefore, all bureaucracies are necessarily political; that is, at the top they must have either traditional or charismatic (i.e., popularly elected) legitimacy. So far, many of the new globalized institutions seem to lack either form. Since globablization is almost by definition anti-traditional, the only alternative would be to invest corporate leaders with the synthetic aura of a charismatic hero. As Surowiecki (2002) suggests, one sign of this manufactured charisma is the rise of the CEO biography as a new genre of management literature, beginning perhaps with the autobiography of former Chrysler head Lee Iacocca (Iacocca 1984, 1988).⁶

Ironically, this loss of control also constitutes a special threat to the very individualist values that were the seed-bed of modern industrial capitalism. In one sense, globalized capitalism is the apotheosis of individualism: that is, jobs are sought and won instead of being ascribed or assigned, job security is uncertain, individual pay is high but "paternalistic" benefits are low, and performance rather than a relationship is demanded of employees. Yet in another sense, individuals as such have become quite disposable and thus of little account: for it is the corporation that survives and controls. Individual workers, individual managers, even individual CEOs come and go, but the corporation (Chrysler, Daimler Chrysler, or perhaps GM-Toyota-Daimler Chrysler-Ford) endures forever.

6.3 Threat and Paranoia

When people experience (or believe they have experienced) a real loss of control over their lives, they are vulnerable to feelings of paranoia, the overspreading sense that all aspects of one's life are controlled by secret powers. According to Janofsky (1995), for example, the "patriot" group E pluribus unum believes that "government officials, especially at the Federal level, are letting constitutional freedoms erode so that rich, powerful leaders of the United Nations can take over the country as part of a plan to create a one-world

---

5 In a later context, Weber criticized the American emphasis upon electing higher-level officials in a bureaucracy, in words that seem prescient as a description of the globalization style of administration: "Such an administrative structure is greatly inferior as a precision instrument to the bureaucratic type with its appointed officials" (Weber, [1922]1968: 267).
6 Recent revelations of failure and fraud on the part of many corporation heads, however, have imperiled the future of this literary genre (Barringer 2003).

government." Thus as one member put it, "Nothing in Government occurs by accident. If it occurs, know that it was planned that way." At the extreme, no detail too insignificant to be left out of their all-embracing mental schemas (cf., Brown 1973), even the yellow fringe on an American flag, for example.[7] People disposed to paranoid views are vulnerable to feeling threatened, hence to authoritarian responses (Sales 1973, Doty, Peterson, & Winter 1991) and thus recruitment by extremist groups across the political spectrum. While it is difficult to get accurate statistical measures, many observers suggest that groups with these beliefs and concerns have been growing in size. In the last few years, for example, the magazine *Paranoia* has expanded its distribution to mainstream supermarket checkout racks.

6.4 Inequality, Sense of Deserving, and Resentment

There is now considerable evidence that globalization increases income inequality both within individual countries as diverse as the United States (Kilborn & Clemetson 2002), China (Smith 2002), Poland (Fisher 2002), and Bolivia (Rohter 2003), and also between nations (Kahn 2002). Salaries of corporate chief executive officers have expanded dramatically (in part through stock options and other accounting maneuvers), both in absolute terms and in relation to salaries of employees at the median or the bottom (Phillips 2002). Nor is this trend confined to profit-making corporations, as suggested by the following typical examples: (1) In December 2002, U.S. President George W. Bush approved $10,000 "bonuses" for top-level political appointees, while at the same time cutting back a pay raise to all federal civil service employees because the government "couldn't afford the cost due to the war on terrorism and post-9/11 national emergency." (2) A few weeks earlier, the nonprofit Educational Testing Service announced year-end bonuses of up to $366,000 to each of its top 15 officers, while cutting back on the nightly beer and snacks for the teachers hired to grade advanced placement exams.[8] (3) And at the University of Michigan over the past 20 years, the salary of the university president has increased from a multiple of about 3.5 times that of an average assistant professor to a multiple of 7 times.

In all these cases, these increasing inequalities are justified by the claim that corporations and nonprofit institutions are simply responding to "market

---

7   For one "analysis" of the yellow-fringed U. S. flag, see "A Military Flag." Retrieved November 10, 2003 from http://www.civil-liberties.com/books/colony5.html
8   See *The New York Times* November 23 and 27, 2002.

forces." Since the market for CEO's or university presidents is a lot tighter than that for line workers or assistant professors, it is presumed necessary to pay whatever the market demands—though in fact exorbitant salaries are often the result of poor oversight by boards of directors and trustees, as well as cozy interlocking relationships between senior officers and boards (see Domhoff 1998). Such justifications depend critically on attributing corporate and institutional successes to the actions of those at the top.[9] Like other cognitions, such attributions are <u>constructed interpretations</u> of events, interpretations that differ across people and are impossible to "prove" definitively. In practice, we often find an asymmetry of attributions (see Abramson, Seligman, & Teasdale 1978, Harvey & Weary 1981, Weiner 1986): CEO's are eager enough to take credit for corporate success, but often they deny failure or blame it on external factors. Such attributional patterns are obviously self-serving to those at the top; further, they are certainly <u>contested</u> and <u>political</u>. ("Risk" and "equity" are also contested concepts that are politically deployed in discussions of corporate compensation structures and controls.)

Whatever their justification, these increasing income inequalities have psychological and political consequences, within and across countries. Under certain conditions, such inequalities increase the sense of relative deprivation among lower-strata workers and countries—especially if these people feel they "deserve" better (see Crosby 1976, also Davies 1969). Depending on whether people externalize or internalize resentment and whether they perceive opportunity for change, relative deprivation can drive a wide variety of different behaviors—from self-improvement to substance abuse to organized violence and rebellion (Crosby 1976). All of these belong in the purview of a political psychology focused on globalization.

Overlaying increased income inequality with ethnic differentiation and stratification can generate an especially explosive effect, because relative deprivation and the sense of deserving are exacerbated by nationalism (see below) and prejudice. As Chua (2002) argues, in many third world countries the market liberalizations associated with globalization—unaltered by the redistributive policies of mature capitalist countries—typically lead to accumulation of wealth by "market dominant minorities"[10] such as the Chinese in the Philippines and

---

9   Surowiecki argues the contrary: "Although it may be hard to believe after a decade and a half of CEO worship, all the available evidence suggests that most chief executives have only a negligible impact on the performance of the companies they run . . . Corporate performance depends far more on what industry a company is in, what proprietary advantages it has, and the general quality of its workforce, than it does on who's at the very top" (2002: 3).

10 In Lewis's terms, "transplanted Westerners and members of Westernized minorities" (1990: 59).

Indonesia, the Croatians in the former Yugoslavia, and the Indians in East Africa.[11] Combined with unrestrained political democracy, the result can be ethnic hatred, turbulence, and violence. Chua applies this model to perceptions and relations across as well as within countries: thus certain countries (typically the United States) can be seen, by many people in other countries, as a kind of global "market dominant minority," attracting hatred from people and countries of a dispossessed—yet "deserving"—third world.

6.5 Skepticism and Malaise about Government

In many parts of the new globalizing economy, things are not going well. Many political, economic, educational, and even cultural institutions show increasing gaps between expectations (or claims) and performance. Even signs of genuine progress can be paralyzed by the resulting states of mind: for example, fatalistic skepticism, cynical exploitation of problems in ways that work to the advantage of corrupt networks of patronage, or (especially on the part of the military) the desire to force the pace by taking over or sweeping away these institutions.

Even in the advanced industrialized countries, signs of political skepticism and malaise can be detected in low voter turnouts (especially among the recently-socialized young people) and absorption in the synthetic celebrity culture of consumption proffered by the media. Political participation—from voluntary "civic" participation to the simple act of voting—then declines.[12] As Patterson argued, "Ordinary citizens have been buffeted by developments they do not control and only vaguely comprehend, and which have diminished their stake, interest, and confidence in elections" (2002: 22). In the United States such declines are most notable among adolescents and young adults (2002: 85-89), the very group that is so extensively involved in the consumer aspects of globalization. When people's social contacts are mediated by mechanisms of mass communication (television, internet), they may be less inclined to develop direct social and political involvement with their neighbors and local community.

With the changes of globalization, the "everyday" becomes disruptively "strange" (see Heitmeyer 1991). One extreme expression of this psychological disruption can be found in the manifesto of Theodore Kaczynski (1995),

---

11 Chua's analysis could easily be extended to other cases such as Saudi resentment of "foreigners" who monopolize technical jobs, or American white men's anger at affirmative action on behalf of women and minorities.
12 Of course this diminished interest on account of lack of comprehension and control is only one of many reasons for voting decline, as Patterson (2002) suggests.

known as the "Unabomber," who argued that industrial capitalism created a sense of psychological and spiritual estrangement:

> The Industrial Revolution and its consequences have been a disaster for the human race. They have . . . destabilized society, have made life unfulfilling, have subjected human beings to indignities, [and] have led to widespread psychological suffering. . . . The continued development of technology will worsen the situation. [paragraph 1]
>
> [Modern industrial] society requires people to live under conditions radically different from those under which the human race evolved and to behave in ways that conflict with the patterns of behavior that the human race developed while living under the earlier conditions. [paragraph 46]

The Unabomber had a political program, no matter how bizarre and unrealistic. Others have responded with more inchoate violence. For example, Timothy McVeigh hit the job market in the 1980s, just as the manufacturing company that had employed his father stopped hiring and moved its blue-collar jobs to other countries. Angry and disappointed at washing out of the army Special Forces school after the Gulf War, he developed paranoid survivalist beliefs that in 1995 led him to blow up the Murrah Federal Building in Oklahoma City. Much more common than the alienated and bitter McVeighs are two other phenomena of bored youth in politically apathetic industrial societies: the "slacker," who dials out of society and plugs into synthetic media, and the "hacker," who disrupts computer and social systems "for the hell of it."[13]

In less advanced countries on the periphery of globalization, the form and effects of malaise may be slightly different. Thus Lewis has described a dreary sequence that too often has played out in the Middle East: "Western-style economic methods brought poverty, Western-style political institutions brought tyranny, even Western-style warfare brought defeat" (1990: 59). Psychologically, these failures have "devalued their traditional values and loyalties and, in the final analysis, robbed them of their beliefs, their aspirations, their dignity, and to an increasing extent even their livelihood" (ibid.). At best, these failures and collapsed identities breed disillusionment and withdrawal; at worst, they fuel a resentful hostility that "turns every disagreement into a problem and

---

13   During the summer of 2000, several large billboards in the Seattle area asked passers-by, "What do you want to destroy today?" In fact, the signs were advertisements for codisk.com, a company specializing in recycling waste from the software industry. It is striking, however, that the ad attracts attention by appealing to the pleasure of destruction—an ominous image, because it reinforces the theme of destruction "just for the hell of it." What may happen when hackers turn to the newly-mapped human genome, or begin to clone deadly viruses?

makes every problem insoluble" (Lewis 1990: 53). The long-term results may include instability, chaos, ethnic hatred and ethno-political warfare, and terrorism.

6.6 Charismatic Nationalism

Threats or devaluation of identities (people's sense of congruence between inner reality and a valued outer "actuality") become a seedbed for the rise of charismatic leaders, according to Erikson's analysis of the appeal of Gandhi (Erikson 1969), Luther (Erikson 1958), and Hitler (Erikson 1950: chap. 9). In such situations, "they have been found and chosen by contemporaries possessed of analogous conflicts and corresponding needs" (Erikson 1964: 204, see also work by Erikson's students and colleagues, for example Albin, Devlin, & Heeger 1980). Thus Lewis observed of people in the Middle East, "It is hardly surprising that so many were willing to listen to voices telling them that the old Islamic ways were best and that their only salvation was to throw aside the pagan innovations of the reformers and return to the True Path that God had prescribed for his people" (1990: 59).

Charismatic leaders come in many different varieties and have many different effects—benign or malignant. Some, like Gandhi, Martin Luther King, Jr., and Nelson Mandela, have led their people to powerful, new, and satisfying identities that engender pride and enable understanding and coping with change. Others, such as Hitler or Osama bin Laden, play upon their followers' resentment, malaise, humiliation, and scorn for the collusion of earlier generations. Offering seductive (but destructive) identities, they recruit followers to new jihads (Rubenstein 2003, describes this sequence in his analysis of the psychological and sociological roots of terrorism).

In response to confusion, anonymity, and the loss of meaning, many people have sought refuge in a renewed commitment to the bounded world with which they are familiar: "place consciousness" (to use a newer word that may be more precise and nuanced than the old term "nationalism"), or "jihad" (Barber's 1995 term, set in opposition to a globalized "McWorld"). The violent forms of jihad are obvious, but milder forms of protest against exclusion from decision-making are also rooted in place consciousness and seek restoration of community, identity, family, and values. For example, Friedman (2001) explained an Irish vote against expanding the European Community in these terms:

> [In Ireland] everyone loves the new roads and economic opportunities, which have enabled Ireland to overcome its legacy of poverty and emigration. Yet many people fear that Ireland's unique emerald landscape and delightfully eccentric culture and

identity could get paved over on this road to paradise... They are becoming more aware of the price.

6.7 Aggression

Aggression, whether in the form of inter-state wars, intra-state ethnopolitical warfare, terrorism, or even such mundane everyday phenomena such as "road rage" (or "airplane rage") may be a kind of "final common path" for many of the psychological-political forces engendered or exacerbated by rapidly-changing forces of globalization that often seem to alter society beyond the comprehension of average people.

6.8 Response of the Globalizers

We must not forget that as people protest and "hack into" the structures of a globalized economy, the global institutions will fight back, by direct, forceful confrontation and/or by elaborating structures of surveillance and repression (Americans have perhaps seen both in the response of the Bush administration to the shock of the September 11, 2001 terror attacks). No doubt there will be searches for the usual suspects and scapegoats: minorities, women, youth, and people who are "different" (perhaps especially with respect to anything involving sexuality or sexual orientation). These, too, become important topics for political psychological investigation.

6.9 The Agenda for Political Psychology

I have suggested that globalization and its political, social, and psychological vicissitudes may be the major trend of the twenty-first century. With roots in two fields at the core of this process (political science and psychology) and links to several other relevant disciplines (sociology, anthropology, history, economics, philosophy), political psychology is uniquely poised to help us understand the problems and issues arising from globalization. Many familiar political psychology concepts will find new or extended application when applied to the issues of globalization: for example, social identity, belief structures, the construction and elaboration of "difference," the appeals of charisma, and aggression. Many of these concepts come together around the topic of equity—that is, what are the relations between outcomes (especially differential outcomes), feelings (of deserving, satisfaction, or resentment), and social-political action (constructive participation versus focused or inchoate aggression)?

Although political psychology and its constituent disciplines may be strategically placed in the academic firmament, they are not likely to be unchanged by this new focus on globalization, for as Sampson suggested, "the postmodern era's postindustrial, information-based, and globally linked social environments will call for a dramatic change in psychology's theories of the person" (1989: 914).

6.10 How Do We Get To This New Agenda?

If the twenty-first century provides political psychologists with plenty of work to do and problems to study, how do we get there from here? That is, what kinds of preparation will best fit the emerging generation of political psychologists for these tasks?

Real-world problems and issues do not come wrapped in neat disciplinary packages. As scholars of a "hybrid" or interdisciplinary field, political psychologists have from the beginning recognized the unique contributions of each of the field's component disciplines to the collective enterprise of political psychology.

6.10.1 What Psychology Can Provide

Psychologists have developed many specific research techniques (experiments, surveys, personality assessment, statistical procedures), as well as a broader concern with methodology. They are well-trained in designing and refining systematic measures, as well as developing innovative ways to measure complex and abstract processes (see, for example, McClelland 1961, and Simonton 1990). Psychologists tend to think in operational terms, recognizing that any "variable" (whatever its verbal definition) is really defined by the particular operations, carried out in particular contexts, that are used to measure it. Such operations may not always be what the researcher imagines them to be. For example, any specific research operation may be more (because it inadvertently introduces extraneous features) or less (because it does not reflect implicit meanings of the concept) than originally imagined by the researcher. Psychologists tend to practice a rather ruthless scrutiny of the validity of measures (their own and those of others), which can be a useful contribution to political psychology research.

6.10.2 What Political Science Can Provide

By itself, however, psychology is not enough. Psychologists are trained to understand social and political phenomena mostly at the individual level, or in terms of universal processes operating only (or mainly) at the individual level. In other words, left to their own devices, psychologists are prone to "psychologizing," or reducing everything to psychological processes and mechanisms. I am often distressed that many of my psychology students (and I don't think mine are unique) seem almost to take delight in their ignorance of history, political science, sociology, and other social science fields. Psychologists need to locate their field in its broader social-historical interdisciplinary contexts.

Because political scientists are trained to think in terms of structure and complexity, they are in a position to correct excessive psychologizing. Structures generate their own dynamics and their own psychological forces, as well as shaping and constraining the expression of individual psychologies. Moreover, political scientists readily grasp the difference between illustrating a relationship (e.g., that certain psychological variables increase or decrease before wars) and explaining an event (e.g., the entire complex of factors that led up to World War I). In contrast, psychologists often focus on statistical significance and neglect effect size or contextual relevance.

6.10.3 Statistics

Both psychologists and political scientists are trained in the use of statistical analysis and inference. Above and beyond furnishing particular techniques, statistics provides a mind-set for the analysis of phenomena that have multiple interacting causes. We recognize that no research finding or even "law" holds true under all conditions and in all situations. There are often exceptions; yet one or even a few exceptions do not necessarily invalidate general conclusions. Statistics teaches us tolerance for these exceptions, telling us how many exceptions we can tolerate before a "finding" is no longer robust. Statistics also sensitizes us to the existence of moderator variables—that is, additional factors acting as contingencies that govern cause-effect relationships. Knowing statistics, political psychologists can decide whether to control additional factors experimentally or statistically. They have access to multivariate techniques for the systematic analysis of complexity.

6.10.4 Beyond Psychology and Political Science

I believe that a truly stimulating and intellectually healthy political psychology will go beyond its two component disciplines, because many other fields can also contribute to our work. For example, historians are well-positioned to call our attention to factors that may slip through the nets of operational definitions. Thus the historian Joll (1968) emphasized the role of "unspoken assumptions"—beliefs, values, heuristics, and working assumptions that are so "obvious" that they do not need to be articulated and, therefore, may not ever appear in official documents or published discursive records. In the case of the outbreak of World War I, for example, such factors include the teachings of Nietzsche and the popularity of an oversimplified Social Darwinism. Historians also remind us that our access to "raw data" is shaped and constrained by processes of memory, recording, and preservation. "The archives" are never a randomly-selected sample of all data, but rather a selection made, preserved, and arranged in accordance with specific principles and often sotto voce political interests (see, for example, Wilson, 1996).

Then too, historians characteristically point out the importance of "accidental" factors that may only apply to a particular event. For example, a full account of how thermonuclear war was avoided during the Cuban Missile Crisis might include the influence of several facts about U.S. President John F. Kennedy: (1) He had actual experience of a world war, including personal combat injury and a brother's death. (2) He had young children. (3) Because of his experience with the bungled Bay of Pigs invasion a year earlier, he had considerable distrust of the recommendations and assurances of military and intelligence officials. (4) Finally, just before the crisis began he had read Tuchman's (1962) book about the accidental escalation to war in 1914, *The Guns of August*. Each of these events might have been ignored by a political scientist or psychologist looking for universal characteristics that can be generalized to all crisis situations; yet each might have contributed some weight to that delicate tipping of the balance away from catastrophe.

The historical perspective may protect both psychology and political science against assuming a false "causal uniqueness" for particular dynamics and mechanisms. Often there are many alternative causal paths that would lead to the same result.

Finally, history can give us perspective on the globalization process, its vicissitudes, and its possible future. Technically, globalization may be multinational and stateless; in many respects, however, it is its own vast empire—a "non-nation-specific form of imperialism" (Scowen 2002: 232). In the past, many other political-economic-social-legal systems also attempted to establish hegemony over a substantial part of the known world: the empires of Rome, Ming China, Spain and the Habsburgs, and Britain, for example. These earlier globalized empires have passed into the discard pile of history, whether from self-limitation (Fairbank 1992: 137-140), the increasing burdens of protecting the imperial periphery (Kennedy 1987), changes in institutions, styles of life, and childrearing that blocked transmission of the requisite psychological qualities to subsequent generations (McClelland 1961: 376-378), and/or the construction and assertion of local identities and counter-structures. Knowing the stories of these past empires may help political psychologists to understand forces at work in the globalized twenty-first century.

Even the humanities can make an important contribution to political psychology. Good writers are like good clinicians: although they may lack (or avoid) experimental techniques, operational definitions, and dazzling statistical analysis, their intuitions and insights into human nature, their understanding of power, sex, and violence, and their insights into the reciprocal relationships of individuals and polities often surpass what we can achieve by more systematic means. Thus the humanities can be a fertile source for insights and hypotheses, which can then be elaborated and tested with more conventional social science techniques of data collection and analysis.

6.10.5 A Plea for Methodological Pluralism

To realize its interdisciplinary inheritance, political psychology needs to be pluralistic, synthetic, and critical. Political psychologists can bring together the best methods and theoretical perspectives of each constituent disciplines and encourage their use in the others. At the same time, their location between disciplines gives them an appropriate caution about method, a sense that every method has its limits and no one method can claim infallibility. For example, many psychologists are strongly committed to experimentation for the perfectly good reason that only experiments enable us to make absolutely certain inferences about causality. Sometimes those inferences aren't so certain, even apart from the philosopher David Hume's warning that we can never be certain about the future. It may turn out that the variable we describe is not exactly the variable that we manipulated, or that we missed a few things or overlooked a few features of an experimental situation.

We often purchase that causal certainty, however, at the price of external validity: the experiments that we construct for the laboratory may not always transport, replicate, and extend themselves to the real world. Thus by themselves, experiments may give a false sense of universalism. Because of their experience of the real world, "real world" practitioners of political psychology are often quick to recognize these problems and thus lament the gap between scholarship and practice. To bridge that gap, all political psychologists must be sensitive to the many different issues and meanings surrounding the concept of "validity." We need to develop alternative methodologies—not instead of, but in addition to experimentation: for example, observation, quasi-experiments, archival exploration, and ethnography.

In the academy, it is rarely easy to bridge (or "transgress") traditional departmental boundaries, policed as they often are by administrators, senior faculty, and journal editors. Even our students, nervously protesting that "we're not history majors" or "this isn't an English class," may question having to read a study of Indian nationalism or Shakespeare's *King Richard I*. To be sure, many interdisciplinary educational ventures do wear out their intellectual welcome, or fission back into their component disciplines (for example, Harvard's Department of Social Relations in the 1960s). On the other hand, new interdisciplinary fields do emerge, adapt, and establish themselves in the curriculum (see Klein 1996), typically by orienting themselves to practical problems. At the curricular level, a related strategy for success may involve focusing our teaching and research efforts on concrete cases, as is done in many professional schools of law, business, and medicine.

Several concrete mechanisms can build bridges across traditional disciplines within individual institutions: cross-listing courses, team teaching, encouraging senior faculty to "take risks," interdisciplinary conferences and "theme semesters." At the national, regional, and international levels, there are professional organizations such as the International Society of Political Psychology and national organizations in the Netherlands and Germany (among other countries), as well as the Political Psychology Divisions of the American Political Science Association and the International Congress of Applied Psychology.

The graduate education of future political psychologists can be enhanced by deliberate "cross-training" procedures—supported by Simonton's (2000) conclusion that creativity results from exposure both to diversifying experiences that help weaken the constraints imposed by conventional socialization, and also to challenging experiences that help strengthen a person's capacity to persevere in the face of obstacles. For example, individual programs or entire institutions could require students to take "cognate" course(s) in another field and have extra-departmental member(s) on prelim and dissertation committees. For ambitious and promising young faculty, there could be fellowships for a year spent mastering some "other" discipline, or "broadening" sabbaticals.

6.11 Conclusion

Political psychology is really a vast interdisciplinary field, far broader than what is implied by the names of its two major constituent disciplines. In this chapter I have argued that our agenda is to be found in the forces of globalization at work in these, the opening decades of the twenty-first century. Our principal task, I suggest, is to develop theory and carry out research that will acknowledge and contribute to enhanced understanding of these global forces and their impact on human society, polity, and psychology.

Our best work is likely to come from the broadest range of sources and inspiration: historical knowledge and perspective, awareness of individual psychological forces, recognition of the realities of structure, intuitive understanding, experience with the scientific method, and skill at statistical analysis. And so it follows that our best scholars and practitioners will be those with the broadest intellectual background, human experience, and professional training.

7 Concluding Remarks: Developments and Trends in Political Psychology

Linda Shepherd

7.1 Overview

The history of political psychology as a subfield is illustrative of the development of any new interdisciplinary effort; the fact that it matured relatively quickly and has grown to the levels indicated in this volume is evidence of the acknowledged importance and relevance of research at the intersection of political and psychological processes. Contributors to this volume have discussed a variety of significant developments as well as important challenges that have emerged over the growth of what is now a transdiscipline known as political psychology. What has become clear is that political psychology was born of necessity; it flourished because it created a unique nexus between two critical fields, which, when combined, had the potential of significantly contributing to a global, cross-cultural understanding of the dynamics of personality in politics.

Political psychology is distinct in that it offers an integrative analysis of political life, combining examination of leadership, political systems, and institutional development with evaluation of psychological processes in political context. As a result, political psychology has been able to open new perspectives in the exploration of political phenomena, human nature, and associated behavior. At its best, political psychology questions the assumptions of both of its parent fields and derives its own principles and conclusions based upon innovative interdisciplinary approaches. The future of this field will be dependent upon its ability to move beyond the boundaries of each of the two parent disciplines to provide dynamic research that will continue to integrate the complexities of human psychology with political action, political institutions, leadership, and public policy.

7.2 Interdisciplinary Successes and Challenges

It is the ability and the willingness of political psychologists to incorporate approaches and subject matter from a variety of disciplines—always directed toward the overarching goal of understanding human beings and their interactions with political processes and outcomes—that enriches the literature produced by political psychologists and expands the importance and utility of their findings. This multidisciplinary emphasis creates opportunities for success and simultaneously presents significant challenges. Those who practice political psychology do not ordinarily have their primary training in political psychology; fields of origin are as diverse as their preferred approaches and methodologies. While the majority of those who conduct research in political psychology have their training in either political science or psychology; specialists in anthropology, sociology, economics, psychiatry, history, as well as other fields, contribute to the growing numbers of scholars who adopt a political psychological approach. As a result, political psychologists have learned to exercise and appreciate a variety of analytic approaches while developing an understanding of the equivalence of many techniques. Working in a multidisciplinary environment also necessitates the development of common terminology and leads to areas of shared knowledge across disciplines as well as the ability to cooperate with those who employ divergent approaches (see Hermann 2002).

As indicated by David Winter (Chapter 6, in this volume), research methods in the field of political psychology have arisen to meet these unique interdisciplinary challenges and have benefited from well-established methodology developed within each of the two parent disciplines. Scholars of political psychology draw from multiple extant methods, using, adapting, or designing one or more to address the specific needs of a particular research effort. These methods may derive from those traditionally used to support research in political behavior, public opinion, psychoanalysis, developmental psychology, cognitive psychology, social psychology, neuroscience, learning theory, linguistics, economics, information processing, or others. Because the methodology of political psychology often combines the literatures of two (or more) disciplines to assess and examine relationships between concepts such as personality, motivation, decision making, leadership, and political behavior among political leaders and across divergent cultures, the researcher may find that necessary methods do not yet exist. The ability to adapt traditional methods, develop new methods, and devise innovative combinations of methods to address research needs has distinguished political psychologists and political psychology. The use of multiple complementary methods in one analysis often increases validity and can enhance context sensitivity. What increasingly interests political psychologists, confronted with a variety of sources *and* several types of relevant information, is the appropriate "triangulation of methods and data" (Hermann 2004: *xvi -xvii)*.

Additionally, as research in political psychology has manifested significant cross-cultural components; scholars have augmented results with the development of comparative models of psychological function and political behavior understood in the context of relevant culture and history. Findings in cultural and psychological anthropology have enhanced cross-cultural studies in political psychology (cf. Renshon and Duckitt 1997, 2000). Cultural, political, and psychological context, when used effectively, concretize abstractions and enhance the validity of conclusions in political psychology. Lasswell warned that "[w]hen the tumultuous life of society is flayed into precedents and tanned into principles, the resulting abstractions suffer a strange fate. They are grouped and regrouped until the resulting mosaic may constitute a logical and aesthetic whole which has long ceased to bear any valid relation to the original reality" (1960, 1). His solution was to recommend a healthy dose of political biography to political psychology as well as the application of "rigorous scrutiny" to the terms of reference upon which each concept relies. The emphasis on contextual elements has assisted in the prevention of invalid abstractions and is prerequisite for valuable insight into individual perspective, self-perception, view of reality, and view of reality in relation to the individual.

Cultural experience influences perception, cognition, affect, motivation, and behavior. Each of these variables develops within a specific cultural dimension. Cultural differences are integral to the study of perceptions, and so will significantly affect any evaluation of the parameters of conflict, framing strategies, and/or policies critical to international negotiations. As Alexander George has noted, from Stalin's misperception of Hitler's motives in 1941 to Khrushchev's mistaken image of Kennedy during the Cuban missile crisis, history abounds with examples of the risks incurred when one harbors incorrect perceptions of the enemy. Accurate analysis and resulting strategy are dependent upon an understanding of the influence of culture, particular memories, and historic events upon the development of "self-image, values, and motivations" (George 2004: *ix)*.

Assumptions of rationality, or indeed irrationality, are often extreme oversimplifications that dangerously ignore the role of culture and its effect upon resulting values and behavioral proclivities (see George 2004, Post 2004). Accordingly, modern investigations into the psychology of terrorism as well as analyses of potential public policy responses to violent nonstate actors have benefited from the interdisciplinary research of political psychologists (cf. Post 2004, Rubenstein 2003). Contemporary realities have forced counterterrorist policies to move beyond simple unitary actor assumptions and to deal with the mix of socialization, ideology, mind-set, self-image, and motivational profiles that describe nonstate actors in specific and divergent cultures.

Political psychology is uniquely situated to contribute to these evolving approaches. The ability of political psychology to draw from multiple disciplinary resources has increased the accuracy and relevance of analyses of political leaders, whether allies or adversaries, and so has benefited related prescriptions for strategy and policy. It is this range of influences on the practice of political psychology that has led to suggestions that the field of political psychology is more aptly viewed as a *perspective* rather than a discipline with strict conceptual or methodological boundaries (McGraw Chapter 2, in this volume, Hermann 2002, Monroe 2002). Political psychology viewed as a perspective is an approach to "understanding politics" that is founded upon "a set of assumptions that serve as consensual premises and scope conditions, indicating the important concepts and ideas that must be covered in any curriculum or training" (Hermann 2002: 46). A perspective in political psychology acknowledges individuals and human nature as important influences on political institutions, systems, and environments; recognizes the importance of values, political events, political environment, cultural and personal context (and others) as influences upon the development of preferences among masses and political elites; includes political process as independent and as dependent variables in studies of political behavior; and enriches research on cognition with theories of motivation and emotion (Hermann 2002). Further, political psychology as a perspective is capable of incorporating "rational choice theory into a broader framework," particularly because political psychology views the self as complex, socially constructed, motivated by loyalties to groups as well as self-interest, characterized by cognitive and affective influences that interact, and composed of multiple identities—both public and private—which shape political behavior and political process (see Monroe 2002).

McGraw has argued that political psychologists should be at the forefront of "the inevitable synthesis between positive political (rational choice) theory and behavioral approaches to judgment and decision making" (Chapter 2, in this volume). Political psychology, from its multidisciplinary perspective, was and is in an ideal position from which to question the assumptions of traditional approaches to both political science and psychology. Political psychology's ability to incorporate cognition and affect into models of political judgment and behavior will assist in illustrating the limitations of rational choice and will contribute to more apt characterizations of decision making.

According to Glad (2002a) the attraction of the rational and scientific in the field of political science was based upon assumptions that research which is scientific should seek general laws which are universally applicable and, that political leaders and decision makers are rational. Many have argued that the drive toward rational scientific inquiry that resulted in predictive theories capable of "grand abstraction" and generalization, were not consistently of utility in the natural sciences, and clearly have limited studies of political leadership and decision making (cf. Glad 2002a, Simon 1985). Political decisions and policies are based upon complex and dynamic processes, understood with reference to context and contingencies. Scholars of political psychology are uniquely trained to undertake research that evaluate these complex phenomena, characterized by the irregularities of the human condition. The mental state, motivation, and intentions of a particular leader remain significant even as they interact with other forces including institutional influences, legal considerations, history, the availability of resources, and the influence of media as well as public opinion (Glad 2002a: 11-17). As Marvick and Glad have here noted "[t]o be truly empirical this science must look at how people actually behave in a variety of situations, noting both the rational and the affective aspects of those choices" (Chapter 3, in this volume).

Scholars in political psychology have had a concerted interest in theories that are capable of describing and predicting the complexities of actual behavior. Along these lines, prospect theory has received some related focus in recent years. Unlike rational choice theory and its emphasis on rational thought and on absolute gains, prospect theory illustrates the subjectivity of decision making, demonstrating that individuals make irrational choices under conditions of threat and possible loss; indeed "losses inflict psychological harm to a greater degree than gains gratify, which means that people are more willing to run risks to avoid or recoup losses than to make gains" (Jervis 2004: 165). Prospect theory predicts that aversion to the threat of loss *and* the attraction of relative gains rather than absolute gains will result in irrational behavior (McDermott 2004, Jervis 2004). The broad implications of this theory led to its inclusion as the subject for several special issues of the journal of *Political Psychology (cf.,* June 1992, April 2004, and June 2004), which featured leaders in political psychology and prospect theory discussing its importance.

The attempt to incorporate human subjectivity into models that will further understanding of psychological and political processes is natural to political psychologists. However, resistance to human subjectivity generally and emotions in particular have roots in the same ancient philosophic tomes that presaged important theories in both political science and psychology. Although the role of emotion has been of great interest to political psychologists in recent years, emotions, passions, and desires were portrayed by Plato as undermining reason and so were rigidly separated; the recommended hierarchy of reason over spirit and desire would be complete and unyielding, whether represented by classes in the just city, or by the tripartite divisions of the soul in the just man. Rule of reason over spirit and emotions would ultimately be the goal of education and of political processes. Current predilections for rational choice were clearly foreshadowed by these ancient arguments for eradicationg the influence of emotions on the individual and in the polis (also see Marcus 2002, 2003).

Lasswell once referred to his groundbreaking book *Psychopathology and Politics,* as an effort that primarily sought "the sophisticating of the political-science audience to the challenge of a new and evolving standpoint for the study of human nature in politics" (1960: 275). Indeed, the goals and concerns of philosophers and theorists from ancient Plato to modern Rawls and beyond are reflected in political psychology. The design of the just society, able to account for and provide checks on human nature while supporting the ability to live well; the creation of a system within which individuals might flourish, the public good might be promoted, and self-rule would ennoble citizens rather than provide a platform for tyranny of the majority—each of these laudable tasks have sparked philosophical debate for millennia. They also represent issues that have been components of research in political psychology since its inception.

George Marcus has stated that "political and moral questions . . . can animate a career and give personal meaning to a professional life" (2002: 97). What does it mean to live well? Which forms of governance best support psychological and material well-being? Answers to questions such as these must speak to the intersection of human nature and politics, as do Robert Lane's recent inquiries into whether democracies can "facilitate cognitive development and emotional maturity" (2002: 382) and whether human development could be "a meaningful crosscultural goal" (2003:781-782). It is clear that political theory will continue to enrich discussions in political psychology, re-emphasizing the importance of the polis to the individual's psychology and examining those interrelationships between optimal psychology and government that are capable of supporting human development. The attempt to define the interplay between politics, morality, philosophy, and human nature can certainly animate a research agenda, and each are vital elements of research in political psychology.

The ubiquitous nature of innovative and multidisciplinary approaches in research devoted to the exploration of relationships between political and psychological phenomena was the genesis for David Winter's argument that the bar is set very high for political psychologists (Chapter 6, in this volume). His contention that the best research in political psychology builds from a wide range of sources including knowledge of history, psychological understanding, political acumen, intuitive understanding, and statistical skill, also led to his assertion: "it follows that our best scholars and practitioners will be those with the broadest intellectual background, human experience, and professional training." These lofty goals, set by and for practitioners of political psychology, that perhaps best explain why the subfield has progressed as far as it has in its short history.

References

Abelson, R.P. 1973. The Structure of Belief Systems. In *Computer Models of Thought and Language* Eds. R. Schank & K.M. Colby, pp. 297-340. San Francisco: W. H. Freeman.

Abelson, R.P. & Carroll, J.D. 1965. Computer Simulation of Individual Belief Systems. *American Behavioral Scientist, 8:* 24-30.

Abramson, L.Y., Seligman, M.E.P., & Teasdale, J.D. 1978. Learned helplessness in humans: Critique and reformulation. *Journal of Abnormal Psychology 87 (1):* 49-74.

Adair, J.G. 2003. May. *The internationalization of psychology.* Invited address to the Western Psychological Association, Vancouver, BC.

Adair, J.G., Puhan, B.N., & Vohra, N. 1993. Indigenization of psychology: Empirical assessment of progress in Indian research. *International Journal of Psychology 28:* 149-169.

Adams, H. 1986. *History of the United States of America During the Administrations of Thomas Jefferson.* New York: Library of America.

Adler, E. 1997. Seizing the Middle Ground: Constructivism in World Politics. *European Journal of International Relations 3:* 319-363.

Albin, M., Devlin, R.J., & Heeger, G. (Eds.). 1980. *New directions in psychohistory: The Adelphi papers in honor of Erik H. Erikson.* Lexington, MA: Lexington Books.

Alexander, M., Brewer, M., & Herrmann, R.K. 1999. Images and Affect: A Functional Analysis of Out-Group Stereotypes. *Journal of Personality and Social Psychology 77:* 78-93.

Alker, H.R. Jr., & Christensen, C. 1972. From Causal Modeling to Artificial Intelligence: The Evolution of a UN Peace-Making Simulation. In *Experimentation and Simulation in Political Science* Eds. J. LaPonce & P. Smoker, pp. 177-223. Toronto: University of Toronto Press.

Alker, H.R. Jr., Duffy, G., Hurwitz, R. & Mallery, J.C. 1991. Text Modeling for International Politics: A Tourist's Guide to Relatus. In *Artificial Intelligence and International Politics* Ed. V.M. Hudson, pp. 97-126. Boulder: Westview.

Alker, H.R., Jr. & Greenberg, W.J. 1977. On Simulating Collective Security Regime Alternatives. In *Thought and Action in Foreign Policy* Eds. G.M. Bonham & M.J. Shapiro. Basel: Birkhauser.

Alliluyeva, S. 1967. *Twenty Letters to a Friend.* New York: Harper and Row.

Altemeyer, B. 1988. *Enemies of freedom: Understanding right-wing authoritarianism.* San Francisco: Jossey-Bass.

Altemeyer, B. 1996. *The authoritarian specter.* Cambridge, MA: Harvard University Press.

Ardila, R. 1996. Political psychology: The Latin American perspective. *Political Psychology 17:* 339-351.

Arian, A. 1996. *Security Threatened.* New York: Cambridge University Press.
Arnett, J.J. 2002. The psychology of globalization. *American Psychologist 57:* 774-783.
Banerjee, S. 1986. Reproduction of Social Structures: An Artificial Intelligence Model. *Journal of Conflict Resolution 30:* 221-252.
Banerjee, S. 1991. Reproduction of Subjects in Historical Structures: Attribution, Identify and Emotion in the Early Cold War. *International Studies Quarterly 35:* 19-37.
Barber, B.R. 1995. *Jihad vs. McWorld.* New York: Times Books.
Barber, J.D. 1985. *The Presidential Character: Predicting performance in the White House.* Englewood Cliffs, New Jersey: Prentice-Hall, Inc.
Barner-Barry, C. & Rosenwein, R. 1985. *Psychological Perspectives on Politics.* Prospect Heights, IL: Waveland Press.
Barringer, F. 2003. Readers, like investors, are tiring of C.E.O.'s. *The New York Times* January 19, Sec. 3: p. 4.
Bar-Tal, D. 2002. The (Social) Psychological Legacy for Political Psychology. In *Political Psychology,* Ed. K.R. Monroe, pp. 173-191. Mahwah, NJ: Erlbaum.
Beer, F.A., Healy A.F. & Bourne Jr., L.E. 2004. Dynamic Decisions: Experimental reactions to war, peace, and terrorism. In *Advances in Political psychology: Volume 1* Ed. M.G. Hermann, pp. 139-167. New York: Elsevier.
Berger, M. 1993. *La folie cachée des hommes de pouvoir.* Paris: Albin Michel.
Bickerton, D. 1981. *Roots of language.* Ann Arbor, MI: Karoma.
Bickerton, D. 1988. Creole languages and the bioprogram. In *Linguistics: The Cambridge survey,* Ed. F. J. Newmeyer, Vol. 2: 267-284. Cambridge: Cambridge University Press.
Blanchard, W. 1984. *Revolutionary Morality: A psychosexual analysis of twelve revolutionists.* Santa Barbara, CA: ABC-Clio.
ter Bogt, T.F.M., Meeus, W.H.J., & Raaijmakers, Q.A.W. 2001. Youth centrism and the formation of political orientations in adolescence and young adulthood. *Journal of Cross-Cultural Psychology 32:* 229-240.
Boulding, E. 2000. A new chance for human peaceableness? *Peace and Conflict: Journal of Peace Psychology 6:* 193-215.
Boulding, K. 1956. *The Image.* Ann Arbor: University of Michigan Press.
Boulding, K. 1959. National Images and International Systems. *Journal of Conflict Resolution* 3: 120-131.
Boyer, P. 2001. *Religion explained: The evolutionary origins of religious thought.* New York: Basic Books.
Brady, H.E., George, A.L., Laver, M., Lupia, A., Munger, M.C., Ostrom, E. & Siverson, R. 2000. The public value of political science research. *PS: Political Science and Politics* (Symposium). *33(1):* 7-64.
Brenner, C. 1974. *An Elementary Textbook of Psychoanalysis.* Revised edition. Garden City, N. J: Doubleday.
Breslauer, G.W. 2002. *Gorbachev and Yeltsin as Leaders.* New York: Cambridge University Press.
Bromberg, N. & Small, V.V. 1983. *Hitler's Psychopathology.* New York: International Universities Press.

Brown, D. 1968. *Against the world: Attitudes of white South Africa.* Garden City, NY: Doubleday.
Brown, R.W. 1973. Schizophrenia, language, and reality. *American Psychologist 28:* 395-403.
Bryder, T. 1986. Political Psychology in Western Europe. In *Political Psychology,* Ed. M.G. Hermann, pp. 434-466. San Francisco: Jossey-Bass.
Burke, J.P. & Greenstein, F.I. 1989. *How Presidents Test Reality: Decisions on Vietnam, 1954 and 1965.* New York: Russell Sage.
Burns, J.M. 1978. *Leadership.* New York: Harper and Row.
Burrows, E.G. & Wallace, M. 1972. The American Revolution: the ideology and psychology of National Liberation. In *Perspectives in American History 6:* 167-306.
Byram, M. & Fleming, M. (Eds.) 1998. *Language learning in intercultural perspective.* Cambridge: Cambridge University Press.
Campbell, J.D., Trapnell, P.D., Heine, S.J., Katz, I.M., Lavallee, L.F., & Lehman, D.R. 1996. Self-concept clarity: measurement, personality correlates, and cultural boundaries. *Journal of Personality and Social Psychology 70:* 141-156.
Caprara, G.V. 2001. Personality and politics: A Congruency theory of impression formation, Self presentation, and political preference. Seminar paper presented at SCASSS, University of Rome "La Sapienza."
Caprara, G.V., Barbaranelli, C., & Zimbardo, P.G. 2002. When parsimony subdues distinctiveness: Simplified public perceptions of politicians' personality. *Political Psychology,* 23: 77-96.
Carbonell, J.G., Jr. 1978. POLITICS: Automated Ideological Reasoning. *Cognitive Science, 2:* 27-51.
Cederman, L. 1997. *Emergent Actors in World Politics: How States and Nations Develop and Dissolve.* Princeton, N.J.: Princeton University Press.
Chandrasekaran, B. 1986. Generic Tasks in Knowledge-Based Reasoning: High Level Building Blocks for Expert System Design. *IEEE Expert 1(3):* 23-30.
Chang, H-C. & Holt, R.G. 1994. A Chinese perspective on face as inter-relational concern. In *The challenge of facework: Cross-cultural and interpersonal issues,* Ed. S. Ting-Toomey, pp. 95-132. Albany: State University of New York Press.
Chirot, D. & Seligman, M.E.P. (Eds.) 2001. *Ethnopolitical warfare: Causes, consequences, and possible solutions.* Washington, DC: American Psychological Association.
Chua, A. 2002. *World on fire: How exporting free market democracy breeds ethnic hatred and global instability.* New York: Doubleday.
Clark, L.P. 1921. Unconscious motives underlying the personalities of Great Statesmen and their relation to epoch-making events: Abraham Lincoln. *Psychoanalytic Review* 8: 1-21.
Clark, L.P. 1923. Unconscious motives underlying the personalities of great statesmen and their relation to epoch-making events: The narcism [sic] of Alexander the Great. *Psychoanalytic Review* 10: 56-69.
Converse, J. 1987. *Survey research in the United States: Roots and emergence.* Berkeley: University of California Press.

Cottam, M. 1994. *Images and Intervention: U.S. Policies in Latin America.* Pittsburgh, PA: University of Pittsburgh Press.
Cottam, R. 1977. *Foreign Policy Motivation.* Pittsburgh, PA: University of Pittsburgh Press.
Crosby, F. 1976. A model of egoistical relative deprivation. *Psychological Review 83:* 85-113.
Dallek, R. 1979. *Franklin D. Roosevelt and American Foreign Policy, 1932-1945.* Oxford: Oxford University Press.
Davies, J.C. 1969. The J-curve of rising and declining satisfactions as a cause of some great revolutions and a contained rebellion. In *The history of violence in America,* Eds. H. D. Graham & T. R. Gurr, pp. 690-729. New York: Praeger.
Dávila, J.M., Fouce, J.G., Gutiérrez, L., Lillo de la Cruz, A., & Martin, E. 1998. La psicología política contemporanea. *Psicología Política* No. 17: 21-43.
De Grazia, S. 1945. A note on the psychological position of the Chief Executive. *Psychiatry 8:* 267-272.
DeNardo, J. 1995. *The Amateur Strategist.* New York: Cambridge University Press.
Deutsch, M. & Kinnvall, C. 2002. "What is Political Psychology?" In *Political Psychology,* Ed. K.R. Monroe, pp.15-42. Mahwah, NJ: Erlbaum.
Dille, B. 2000. The Prepared and Spontaneous Remarks of Presidents Reagan and Bush: A Validity Comparison for At-a-Distance Measurements. *Political Psychology* 21(3): 573-585.
Dille, B. & Young, M.D. 2000. The Conceptual Complexity of Presidents Carter and Clinton: An Automated Content Analysis of Temporal Stability and Source Bias. *Political Psychology 21(3):* 587-597.
DiRenzo, G.J. 1974. *Personality and Politics.* Garden City, NY: Anchor Press, Doubleday.
Domhoff, G.W. 1998. *Who rules America? Power and politics in the year 2000.* Mountain View, CA: Mayfield Pub. Co.
Dorna, A. 1998. Presencia y realidad de la psicología política francesa. *Psicología Política* No. 16: 49-73.
Doty, R.M., Peterson, B.E., & Winter, D.G. 1991. Threat and authoritarianism in the United States, 1978-1987. *Journal of Personality and Social Psychology 61:* 629-640.
Driver, M.J. 1977. Individual differences as determinants of aggression in the Inter Nation Simulation. In *A Psychological Examination of Political Leaders,* Ed. M.G. Hermann, pp. 337-353. New York: Free Press.
Duffy, G. & Tucker, S.A. 1995. Political Science: Artificial Intelligence Applications. *Social Science Computing Review 13:* 1-21.
Eisenhower, D.D. 1967. *At Ease: Stories I tell my friends.* New York: Doubleday.
Elms, A.C. 1976. *Personality in Politics.* New York: Harcourt Brace Jovanovich.
Erikson, E.H. 1950. *Childhood and society.* New York: Norton.
Erikson, E.H. 1959. *Identity and the Life Cycle.* New York: International Universities Press.
Erikson, E.H. 1962 [1958]. *Young man Luther.* New York: Norton.
Erikson, E.H. 1964. *Insight and responsibility.* New York: Norton.
Erikson, E.H. 1969. *Gandhi's Truth.* New York: Norton.

Erikson, R., Mackuen, M. & Stimson, J. 2002. *The Macro Polity.* New York: Cambridge University Press.
Estes, T. 2001. The art of Presidential Leadership: George Washington and the Jay Treaty. V*irginia Magazine of History and Biography 109:* 126-158.
Fairbank, J.K. 1992. *China: A new history.* Cambridge, MA: Harvard University Press.
Feldman, O. 1990. Political Psychology in Japan. *Political Psychology 11*: 787-804.
Feldman, O. 1997. Culture, society, and the individual: Cross-cultural political psychology in Japan. *Political Psychology 18,* 327-353.
Feldman, O. 2000. *The Japanese political personality: Analyzing the motivations and culture of freshman Diet members.* New York: St. Martin's.
Feldman, O., & Valenty, L.O. (Eds.) 2001. *Profiling political leaders: Cross-cultural studies of personality and behavior.* Westport, CT: Praeger.
Feldman, O., & De Landtsheer, C. (Eds.) 1998. *Politically speaking: A worldwide examination of language used in the public sphere.* Westport, CT: Praeger.
Fenichel, O. 1945. *The Psychoanalytic theory of neurosis.* New York: Norton.
Fisher, I. 2002. As Poland endures hard times, capitalism comes under attack. *The New York Times,* June 12, p. A1.
Fiske, A.P. 2002. Using individualism and collectivism to compare cultures: A critique of the validity and measurement of the constructs: Comment on Oyserman et al. (2002). *Psychological Bulletin, 128:* 78-98.
Fiske, A.P., & Tetlock, P.E. 1997. Taboo trade-offs: Reactions to transactions that transgress the spheres of justice. *Political Psychology 18:* 255-297.
Fiske, D.W., & Maddi, S.R. 1961. *Functions of varied experience.* Homewood, IL: Dorsey.
Flügel, J.C. 1947 [1920]. On the character and married life of Henry VIII. In *Men and their Motives.* New York: International Universities Press.
Freedman, A.E. & P.E. Freedman. 1975. *The Psychology of Political Control.* New York: St. Martin's Press.
Freud, A. 1937. *The Ego and the mechanisms of defense.* London: International Universities Press.
Freud, S. 1912. *Totem and Taboo.* Standard Edition of the Complete Psychological Works of Sigmund Freud, 13: 1-161.
Freud, S. & Bullitt, W.C. 1966. *Thomas Woodrow Wilson, A Psychological Study.* Cambridge, MA: Houghton Mifflin..
Friedman, T.L. 2001. The Lexus and the shamrock. *The New York Times,* August 3, p. A25.
Funk, C.L. & Sears, D.O. 1991. Are we Reaching Undergraduates? A Survey of Course Offerings in Political Psychology. *Political Psychology 12:* 559-572.
George, A. 2004. Foreword. In *Leaders and their followers in a dangerous world.* J.M. Post, pp. ix-xiii. Ithaca: Cornell University Press.
George, A. 1969. The 'operational code': a neglected approach to the study of political leaders and decision-making. *International Studies Quarterly 23:* 190-222.
George, A.L. & George. J.L. 1956. *Woodrow Wilson and Colonel House: A Personality Study.* New York: Dover.

Gibson, J. & Gouws, A. 2002. *Overcoming Intolerance in South Africa*. New York: Cambridge University Press.
Giles, M.W., Mizell, F., & Patterson, D. 1989. Political Scientists' Journal Evaluations Revisited. *PS: Political Science and Politics*. September.
Gilpin, R. 2000. *The challenge of global capitalism: The world economy in the 21st century*. Princeton, NJ: Princeton University Press
Glad, B. 1983. Black-and-white Thinking: Ronald Reagan's approach to foreign policy. *Political Psychology* 4: 33-76.
Glad, B. 1986. *Key Pittman: the tragedy of a Senate insider*. New York: Columbia University Press.
Glad, B. 1989. Personality, political and group process variables in foreign policy decision-making: Jimmy Carter's handling of the Iranian Hostage Crisis. *International Political Science Review* 10: 35-61.
Glad, B. 1996. Passing the baton: transformational political leadership from Gorbachev to Yeltsin; from de Klerk to Mandela. *Political Psychology* 17: 1-28.
Glad, B. 1999. Yeltsin and the new political [dis]order. In *The Russian Transformation*, Eds. B. Glad and E. Shiraev. New York: St. Martin's Press.
Glad, B. 2000. When governments are good. In *The Moral Authority of Government: Essays to Commemorate the Centennial of the National Institute of Social Sciences*, Eds. M. Kennedy, R.G. Hoxie, B. Repland. New Brunswick, N.J.: Transaction.
Glad, B. 2002a. Political leadership: some methodological considerations. In *Political Leadership for the New Century: Personality and Behavior among American Leaders*, Eds. L.O. Valenty and O. Feldman. Westport, CT: Praeger.
Glad, B. 2002b. Why tyrants go too far: malignant narcissism and absolute power. *Political Psychology* 23: 1-39.
Glad, B. 2003a. Bill Clinton: Character and decision making. In *The Clinton Presidency*. Little Rock: University of Arkansas Press.
Glad, B. 2003b. When Presidents are Tough. In *The Annual of Psychoanalysis*, Vol. 31. Chicago: The Analytic Press.
Glad, B. & Link, M. 1996. President Nixon's inner circle of advisers. *Presidential Studies Quarterly, 26:* 13-40.
Glad, B. & Shiraev, E. 1999a. The reformer in office. In *The Russian Transformation*, Eds. B. Glad and E. Shiraev. New York: St. Martin's Press.
Glad, B. & Shiraev, E. 1999b. A profile of Mikhail Gorbachev: Psychological and sociological underpinnings. In *The Russian Transformation*, Eds. B. Glad and E. Shiraev. New York: St. Martin's Press.
Goldhamer, H. 1978. *The Adviser*. New York: Elsevier.
Gorer, G. 1943. Themes in Japanese culture. *Transactions of the New York Academy of Sciences* Ser. II:5, 106-24.
Gorer, G. & Rickman, J. 1949. *The People of Great Russia: A psychological study*. London: Cresset.
Graber, D. 2004. Mediated Politics and Citizenship in the Twenty-First Century. *Annual Review of Psychology 55:* 545-71.
Greenstein, F.I. 1960. The Benevolent Leader: Children's Images of Political Authority. *American Political Science Review, 54:* 934-943.

Greenstein, F.I. 1968. Private order and the public order: A proposal for collaboration between psychoanalysts and political scientists. *Psychoanalytic Quarterly 37:* 261-81.
Greenstein, F.I. 1969. *Personality and Politics: Problems of evidence, inference and conceptualization.* New York: Markham.
Greenstein, F.I. 1982. *The hidden hand Presidency: Eisenhower as leader.* New York: Basic Books.
Greenstein, F.I. 1987. *Personality and Politics: Problems of Evidence, Inference and Conceptualization.* Princeton: Princeton University Press.
Hagerty, J.C. 1983. *The Diary of James C. Hagerty: Eisenhower in midcourse.* Bloomington: University of Indiana.
Haidt, J., Koller, S.H., & Dias, M.G. 1993. Affect, culture, and morality, or is it wrong to eat your dog? *Journal of Personality and Social Psychology 65:* 613-628.
Hardt, M., & Negri, A. 2000. *Empire.* Cambridge, MA: Harvard University Press.
Hartmann, H. 1958. *Ego Psychology and the problem of adaptation.* New York: International Universities Press.
Harvey, J. H., & Weary, G. 1981. *Perspectives on attributional processes.* Dubuque, IA: W.C. Brown.
Hastie, R. 1988. A Computer Simulation Model of Person Memory. *Journal of Experimental Social Psychology 24:* 423-447.
Heine, S.J. & Lehman, D.R. 1997. Culture, dissonance, and self-affirmation. *Personality and Social Psychology Bulletin 23:* 389-400.
Heine, S.J., Lehman, D.R., Markus, H.R., & Kitayama, S. 1999. Is there a universal need for positive self-regard? *Psychological Review 106:* 766-794.
Heitmeyter, W. 1991. Wenn der Alltag fremd wird: Modernisierungsshock und Fremdenfeinlichkeit [When the familiar becomes strange: Modernization shock and aversion toward the strange]. *Blätter für deutsche und internationale Politik 36:* 851-858.
Held, J. (Ed.) 1993. *Democracy and right-wing politics in Eastern Europe in the 1990s.* Boulder, CO: East European Monographs.
Hermann, M.G. 1980. Examining the Foreign Policy Behavior Using the Personal Characteristics of Political Leaders. *International Studies Quarterly 24(1):* 7-46.
Hermann, M.G. 1984. Personality and foreign policy decision making: A study of 53 heads of government. In *Foreign policy decision-making: Perceptions, cognition, and artificial intelligence* Ed. D. A. Sylvan and S. Chan, 53-80. New York: Praeger.
Hermann, M.G. (Gen. Ed.) 1986. *Political psychology: Contemporary problems and issues.* San Francisco: Jossey-Bass.
Hermann, M.G. 1987. Assessing the foreign policy role orientations of sub-Saharan African leaders. In *Role theory and foreign policy analysis* Ed. S.G. Walker, pp. 161-198. Durham, NC: Duke University Press.
Hermann, M.G. 2002. Political Psychology as a Perspective in the Study of Politics. In *Political Psychology,* Ed. K.R. Monroe, pp. 43-60. Mahwah, NJ: Erlbaum.
Hermann, M.G. (Ed.) 2004. *Advances in Political psychology: Volume 1.* New York: Elsevier.

Hermann, M.G. & Hermann, C.F. 1989. Who makes foreign policy decisions and how: An empirical inquiry. *International Studies Quarterly* 33: 361-388.
Hermann, M.G. & Milburn, T. (Ed.) 1977. *A Psychological examination of political leaders.* New York : Free Press.
Herrmann, R.K. & Fischerkeller, M. 1995. Beyond the Enemy Image and Spiral Model: Cognitive-Strategic Research after the Cold War. *International Organization 49(3):* 415-450.
Herrmann, R.K., Voss, J.F., Schooler, T.Y.E. & Ciarrochi, J. 1997. Images in International Relations: An Experimental Test of Cognitive Schemata. *International Studies Quarterly 41:* 403-433.
Herrmann, R.K., Tetlock, P. & Visser, P. 1999. Mass Public Decisions to Go to War: A Cognitive-Interactionist Perspective. *American Political Science Review 93:* 553-573.
Hibbing, J. & Theiss-Morse, E. 1995. *Congress as Public Enemy.* New York: Cambridge University Press.
Hibbing, J. & Theiss-Morse, E. (Eds.). 2001. *What is it About Government that Americans Dislike?* New York: Cambridge University Press.
Hibbing, J. & Theiss-Morse, E.. 2002. *Stealth Democracy.* New York: Cambridge University Press.
Ho, D.Y.F. 1976. On the Concept of Face. *American Journal of Sociology 81:* 867-884.
Holsti, O.R. 1967. Cognitive Dynamics and Images of the Enemy. *Journal of International Affairs XXI:* 16-39.
Holsti, O.R. 1990. Crisis management. In *Psychological dimensions of war* Ed. B. Glad. Newbury Park, UK: Sage Publications
Holsti, O.R. 1992. Public Opinion and Foreign Policy: Challenges to the Almond-Lippmann Consensus. *International Studies Quarterly 36:* 439-466.
Holsti, O.R. 1996. *Public Opinion and American Foreign Policy.* Ann Arbor: University of Michigan Press.
Hong, Y., Morris, M. W., Chiu, C, & Benet-Martinez, V. 2000. Multicultural minds: A dynamic constructivist approach to culture and cognition. *American Psychologist 55:* 709-720.
Hopf, T. 1998. The Promise of Constructivism in International Relations Theory. *International Security 23 (1):* 171-200.
Hopf, T. 2002. *Social Construction of International Politics. Identities and Foreign Policies, Moscow 1955 and 1999.* Ithaca: Cornell University Press.
Huckfeldt, R. & Sprague, J. 1995. *Citizens, Politics, and Social Communication.* New York: Cambridge University Press.
Hudson, V.M. (Ed.) 1991a. *Artificial Intelligence and International Politics,* Westview Press, Boulder, CO.
Hudson, V.M. 1991b. Scripting International Power Dramas: A Model of Situational Predisposition. In *Artificial Intelligence and International Politics* Ed. V.M. Hudson, pp. 194-220. Westview Press, Boulder, CO.
Hunt, L. 1992. *The Family Romance of the French Revolution.* Berkeley: University of California Press.
Hunt, W.B. 1997. *Getting to war: Predicting international conflict with mass media indicators.* Ann Arbor: University of Michigan Press.

Huntington, S.P. 1993. The clash of civilizations? *Foreign Affairs 72:* 22-49.
Iacocca, L.A. (with W. Novak) 1984. *Iacocca: An autobiography.* New York: Bantam Books.
Iacocca, L.A. 1988. *Talking straight.* New York: Bantam Books.
Iyengar, S. & McGuire, W. J. (Eds.). 1993. *Explorations in Political Psychology.* Durham, NC: Duke University Press.
Iyengar, S. & Simon, A.F. 2000. New Perspectives and Evidence on Political Communication and Campaign Effects. *Annual Review of Psychology 51:* 149-16
Janis, I.L. 1972. *Victims of Groupthink: A Psychological Study of Foreign-policy Decisions and Fiascoes.* Boston: Houghton Mifflin Co.
Janofsky, M. 1995. Demons and conspiracies haunt a "patriot" world. *The New York Times,* May 31, p. A18.
Jefferson, T. 1983. *Jefferson's extracts from the Gospels: "The philosophy of Jesus" and "The life and morals of Jesus,"* (Ed.) D.W. Adames. Princeton: Princeton University Press.
Jefferson, T. 1950-. *The Papers of Thomas Jeferson.* Vols. 1-27 to date. Ed. J. Boyd, C.T. Cullen, J. Catanzariti, & B.B. Oberg. Princeton: Princeton University Press.
Jervis, R. 1976. *Perception and misperception in international politics.* Princeton, N.J.: Princeton University Press,
Jervis, R. 1989. Political Psychology: Some Challenges and Opportunities. *Political Psychology 10:* 481-493.
Jervis, R. 1994. Political implications of loss aversion: The Iranian hostage rescue mission. In *Avoiding losses/taking risks: Prospect theory and international conflict,* Ed. B. Farnham. Ann Arbor, MI: University of Michigan Press.
Jervis, R. 1997. *System Efects: Complexity in Political and Social Life.* Princeton: Princeton University Press.
Jervis, R. 2004. The implications of prospect theory for human nature and values. *Political Psychology 25:* 163-176.
Job, B.L. & Johnson, D. 1991. UNCLESAM: The Application of a Rule-Based Model of U.S. Foreign Policy Making. In *Artificial Intelligence and International Politics,* Ed. V.M. Hudson. Westview Press, Boulder, CO.
Joll, J. 1968. *1914: The unspoken assumptions.* London: Weidenfeld & Nicolson.
Jones, E. 1951. Evolution and revolution. In *Essays in applied psychoanalysis, 1:* 254-275. London: Hogarth.
Jones, E. 1913. The Case of Louis Bonaparte, King of Holland. *Journal of Abnormal Psychology 8:* 289-310.
Jones, E.E., & Harris, V.A. 1967. The attribution of attitudes. *Journal of Experimental Social Psychology 3:* 1-24.
Jutras, H. 1995. *Québec is killing me.* Ottawa, Canada: Golden Dog Press.
Kaczynski, T. 1995. *Industrial society and its future* [the "Unabomber manifesto]. Retrieved November 10, 2003 from http://www.panix.com/~clays/Una/
Kahn, J. 2002. Losing faith: Globalization proves disappointing. *The New York Times,* March 21, p. A8.
Kahneman, D., Slovic, P., & Tversky, A. 1982. (Eds.) *Judgment under Uncertainty: Heuristics and Biases.* New York: Cambridge University Press.

Kahneman, D. & Tversky, A. 1979. Prospect Theory: An Analysis of Decision under Risk. *Econometrica 47:* 263-291.
Kaplan, R.D. 1996. *The ends of the earth: A journey at the dawn of the 21st century.* New York: Random House.
Kauffman, S. 1995. *At Home in the Universe: the Search for Laws of Self-Organization and Complexity.* Oxford: Oxford University Press.
Kawata, J. & Araki, Y. 2003. *Handbook of Political Psychology.* Tokyo: Hokuju Shuppan.
Kearns Goodwin, D. 1976. *Lyndon Johnson and the American Dream.* New York: Harper Row.
Kearns Goodwin, D. 1987. *The Fitzgeralds and the Kennedys.* New York: Simon and Schuster.
Kennedy, P.M. 1987. *The rise and fall of the great powers: Economic change and military conflict from 1500 to 2000.* New York: Random House.
Khong, Y.F. 1992. *Analogies at war: Korea, Munich, Dien Bien Phu, and Vietnam decisions of 1965.* Princeton, NJ: Princeton University Press.
Kilborn, P.T. & Clemetson, L. 2002. Gains of 90's did not lift all, census shows. *The New York Times,* June 5, pp. 1, 20.
Kille, K.J. & Scully, R.M. 2003. Executive heads and the role of intergovernmental organizations: Expansionist leadership in the United Nations and the European Union. *Political Psychology 24:* 175-198.
Kimmel, P. 1994. Cultural perspectives on international negotiations. *Journal of Social Issues 50:* 179-196.
Kinder, D.R. 1998. Opinion and Action in the Realm of Politics. In *The Handbook of Social Psychology* (4th Edition) Eds. D.T. Gilbert, S.T. Fiske, & G. Lindzey. New York: McGraw Hill.
Kitts, K. & Glad, B. (in press). Sidestepping the hawks: Eisenhower, The Solarium Study and the Hungarian Crisis of 1956. In *The Art of Political Leadership* Ed. Larry Berman. New York: Rowman & Littlefield.
Klandermans, B., Sabucedo, J.M., Rodriguez, M., & de Weerd, M. 2002. Identity processes in collective action participation: Farmers' identity and farmers' protest in the Netherlands and Spain. *Political Psychology 23:* 235-251.
Klein, J.T. 1996. *Crossing boundaries: Knowledge, disciplinarities, and interdisciplinarities.* Charlottesville, VA: University of Virginia Press.
Knollenberg, B. 1968 [1940]. *Washington and the revolution: A reappraisal.* New York: Archon.
Knutson, J.N. (Ed.) 1973. *Handbook of Political Psychology.* San Francisco: Jossey-Bass.
Kohut, H. 1977. *The Restoration of the Self.* Madison, WI: International Universities Press.
Kohut, H. 1985. *Self-psychology and the Humanities.* New York: Norton.
Kohut, H. 1991. *The search for the self: Selected writings of Heinz Kohut: 1978-1981.* Vol. 4. Ed. Paul Ornstein. Madison: CT: International Universities Press.
Kohut, T. 1991. *Wilhelm I and the Germans: A study in leadership.* New York: Oxford University Press.
Kolodner, J.L. 1991. Improving Human Decision Making through Case-Based Decision Aiding. *AI Magazine,12(2):* 52-68.

Kolodner, J.L. 1993. *Case-Based Reasoning.* San Mateo, CA: Morgan Kaufmann Publishers.
Kossowska, M., & Van Hiel, A. 2003. The relationship between need for closure and conservative beliefs in Western and Eastern Europe. *Political Psychology 24:* 501-518.
Kressel, N.J. 1993. *Political Psychology: Classic and Contemporary Readings.* New York: Paragon House.
Krosnick, J. A. 2002. Is political psychology sufficiently psychological? Distinguishing political psychology from psychological political science. In *Thinking about political psychology* Ed. J. Kuklinski. New York: Cambridge University Press.
Krosnick, J.A. & M.G. Hermann. 1993. Report on the 1991 Ohio State University Summer Institute in Political Psychology. *Political Psychology 14:* 363-373.
Krosnick, J.A. & K.M. McGraw. 2002. Psychological Political Science versus Political Psychology True to its Name: A Plea for Balance. In *Political Psychology* Ed. K.R. Monroe, pp. 79-94. Mahwah, NJ: Erlbaum.
Kuklinski, J.H. (Ed.). 2001. *Citizens and Politics: Perspectives from Political Psychology.* New York: Cambridge University Press.
Kuklinski, J.H. (Ed.). 2002. *Thinking about Political Psychology.* New York: Cambridge University Press.
Lamare, J.W. & Milburn, T.W. 1990. Political Psychology in New Zealand. *Political Psychology 11:* 607-616.
Lane, R.E. 1962. *Political ideology.* New York: Free Press.
Lane, R.E. 2002. Turning political psychology upside down. In *Political Psychology* Ed. K.R. Monroe, pp. 367-384. Mahwah, NJ: Erlbaum.
Lane, R.E. 2003. Rescuing political science from itself. In *Handbook of Political Psychology* (Eds.) Sears, D.O., Huddy, L. & Jervis, R., pp. 755-793. New York: Oxford University Press.
Langer, W.C. 1972[1943]. *The Mind of Adolf Hitler: The Secret Wartime Report.* New York: Basic Books.
Laslett, P. 1996. *A fresh map of life: The emergence of the third age.* 2nd Ed. Houndmillls, Basisngstoke, Hampshire: Macmillan.
Lasswell, H.D. 1965. The study of political elites. In *World Revolutionary Elites: Studies in Coercive Ideological Movements* Eds. H.D. Lasswell & D. Lerner, pp. 3-28. Cambridge: Harvard University Press.
Lasswell, H.D. 1960[1930]. *Psychopathology and politics: with afterthoughts by the author.* New York: Viking Press.
Lasswell, H.D. 1951. *The World Revolution of Our Time: A Framework for Basic Policy Research.* Stanford: Stanford Universitiy Press.
Lasswell, H.D. 1948. *Power and personality.* New York, W. W. Norton.
Lasswell, H.D. 1936. *Politics: Who gets what, when, how.* New York: McGraw-Hill.
Lasswell, H.D. 1930. *Psychopathology and politics.* Chicago: University of Chicago Press.
Lasswell, H.D. 1927. Types of political personalities. *Proceedings of the American Sociological Society, 22:* 150-169.

Lau, R.R. & Sears, D.O. (Eds.) 1986. *Political Cognition*. Hillsdale, NJ: Erlbaum.
Lebow, R.N. 1981. *Between peace and war: The nature of international crisis*. Baltimore: Johns Hopkins University Press.
Lehman, D.R. (Ed.) 1993. Psychological research on the Persian Gulf War. Special Issue, *Journal of Social Issues 49*, No. 4.
Lehman, D.R., Chiu, C-Y., & Schaller, M. 2004 (in press). Psychology and culture. *Annual Review of Psychology, 54*.
Leites, N. 1951. *The operational code of the Politburo*. New York: McGraw-Hill.
Leites, N.C. 1971. *The new ego: pitfalls in current thinking about patients in psychoanalysis*. New York: Science House.
Leites, N. 1977. *Psychopolitical analysis: Selected writings of Nathan Leites*. Ed. E.W. Marvick. New York: Wiley.
Leites, N. 1988. *Soviet Style in War*. New York: Crane, Russack.
Leites, N. & Kecskemeti, P. 1947-48. Some psychological hypotheses on Nazi Germany. *Social Psychology 26*:141-83; *27*:91-117; 241-70; *28*:141-64.
Levi, A., & Tetlock, P.E. 1980. A Cognitive Analysis of Japan's 1941 Decision for War. *Journal of Conflict Resolution 24:* 195-211.
Levin, S. 2000. Undergraduate Education in Political Psychology. *Political Psychology 21:* 603-620.
Lewin, K. 1936. *Principles of Topological Psychology*. New York: McGraw-Hill.
Lewis, B. 1990. The roots of Muslim rage. *The Atlantic Monthly*, September, pp. 47-60. (Abridged reprinting in C. Kegley, Ed., *The new global terrorism: Characteristics, causes, controls*, pp. 194-201. Upper Saddle River, NJ: Prentice Hall.)
Link, M.W. & Glad, B. 1994. Exploring the Psychopolitical Dynamics of Advisory Relations: The Carter Administration's 'Crisis of Confidence." *Political Psychology 15(3):* 461-480.
Lodge, M. & McGraw, K.M. (Eds.) 1995. *Political Judgment: Structure and Process*. Ann Arbor: University of Michigan Press.
Loewenheim, F.L., Langley, H., & Jonas, M. (Eds.) 1975. *Roosevelt and Churchill, Their secret wartime correspondence*. New York: Saturday Review Press.
Lupia, A. 2000. Evaluating Political Science Research: Information for Buyers and Sellers. *PS: Political Science and Politics 33:* 7-14.
Lupia, A. & McCubbins, M.D. 1998. *The Democratic Dilemma: Can Citizens Learn what They Need to Know?* New York: Cambridge University Press.
Lupia, A., McCubbins, M.D. & Popkin, S.L. (Eds.) 2000. *Elements of Reason*. New York: Cambridge University Press.
Lynn, K. 1977. *A divided people*. Contributions in American studies #30. Westport CT: Greenwood Press.
Macdonald, S. 2000. *Rolling the iron dice: Historical analogies and decisions to use military force in regional contingencies*. Westport, CT: Greenwood.
Mackenzie, W.J.M. & Robins, K. (Eds.) 1960. *Five elections in Africa*. London: Oxford University Press.
Mallery, J.C. 1991. Semantic Content Analysis: A New Methodology for the Relatus Natural Language Environment. In *Artificial Intelligence and International Politics* Ed. V.M. Hudson, pp. 347-385. Boulder: Westview.

Marcus, G.E. 2002. Political Psychology: A Personal View. In *Political Psychology* Ed. K.R. Monroe, pp. 95-106. Mahwah, NJ: Erlbaum.
Marcus, G.E. 2003. The Psychology of Emotion and Politics. In *Handbook of Political Psychology* Eds. Sears, D.O., Huddy, L. & Jervis, R., pp. 182-221. New York: Oxford University Press.
Marcus, G., Sullivan, J., Theiss-Morse, E. & Wood, S. 1995. *With Malice Toward Some: How People Make Civil Liberties Judgments.* New York: Cambridge University Press.
Marfleet, B.G. 2000. The Operational Code of John F. Kennedy During the Cuban Missile Crisis: A Comparison of Public and Private Rhetoric. *Political Psychology 21(3):* 545-558.
Marvick, E.W. 1983. Favorites in Early Modern Europe: A recurrent psychopolitical role. *Journal of Psychohistory 10:* 463-489.
Marvick, E.W. 1986. *Louis XIII: The making of a king.* New Haven: Yale University Press.
Marvick, E.W. 1997a. Thomas Jefferson's personality and his politics. *Psychohistory Review 25:* 127-164.
Marvick, E.W. 1997b. Beyond the narcissistic leader: Toward comparing psychopolitical roles. *Mind and Human Interaction 8:* 62-81.
Marvick, E.W. 2000. Family Imagery and Revolutionary Spirit: Washington's Creative Leadership. In *George Washington and the Origins of the American Presidency* Eds. M.J. Rozell, W.D. Pederson, & F.J. Williams, pp. 77-92. Westport, CT: Praeger.
Marvick, E.W. 2001. Sex, politics, and the psychobiographer, with remarks on the case of Jefferson. *Clio's Psyche 8:* 105-116.
Marvick, E.W. 2002. Half a century of childhood. *Clio's Psyche 9:* 1-36.
Masuda, T. & Nisbett, R. 2001. Attending holistically versus analytically: Comparing the context sensitivity of Japanese and Americans. *Journal of Personality and Social Psychology 81,* 922-934.
McClelland, D.C. 1961. *The achieving society.* Princeton, NJ: Van Nostrand.
McDermott, R. 1994. Prospect theory in international relations: The Iranian hostage rescue mission. In *Avoiding losses/taking risks: Prospect theory and international conflict,* Ed. B. Farnham. Ann Arbor, MI: University of Michigan Press.
McFarland, S., Ageyev, V.S. & Abalakina-Paap, M.A. 1992. Authoritarianism in the former Soviet Union. *Journal of Personality and Social Psychology 63:* 1004-1010.
McGraw, K.M. 2000. Contributions of the Cognitive Approach to Political Psychology. *Political Psychology 21:* 805-832.
McGuire, William J. 1969. The Nature of Attitudes and Attitude Change. In *Handbook of Social Psychology* (2nd edition), Eds. G. Lindzey & E. Anderson. Reading, MA: Addison-Wesley.
McGuire, W.J. 1983. A Contextualist Theory of Knowledge: Its Implications for Innovation and Reform in Psychological Research. In *Advances in Experimental Social Psychology* (Vol. 16) Ed. L. Berkowitz. New York: Academic Press.
McGuire, W.J. 1993. The Poly-Psy Relationship: Three Phases of a Long Affair. In *Explorations in Political Psychology* Eds. S. Iyengar & W.J. McGuire. Durham: Duke University Press.

Meredith, M. 1998. *Nelson Mandela*. New York: St Martin's Press.
Messer-Davidow, E. Shumway, D.R., & Sylvan, D.J. 1993. (Eds.) *Knowledges: Historical and Critical Studies in Disciplinarity*. Charlottesville, VA: University Press of Virginia.
Michener, J.A. 1983. *Poland*. New York: Random House.
Micklethwait, J. & Wooldridge, A. 2000. *A future perfect: The essentials of globalization*. New York: Crown Business.
Milburn, T. & Christie, D.J. 1990. Effort justification as a motive for continuing war. In *Psychological Dimensions of War* Ed. B. Glad. Newbury Park, CA: Sage Publications.
Miller, J. 2002. Bringing culture to basic psychological theory—Beyond individualism and collectivism: Comment on Oyserman et al. (2002). *Psychological Bulletin 128:* 97-109.
Miller, J.G. & Bersoff, D.M. 1992. Culture and moral judgment: How are conflicts between justice and interpersonal responsibilities resolved? *Journal of Personality and Social Psychology 62:* 541-554.
Mishal, S. & Morag, N. 2002. Political expectations and cultural perceptions in the Arab-Israeli peace negotiations. *Political Psychology 23:* 325-353.
Moghaddam, F.M. & Crystal, D.S. 1997. Revolutions, samurai, and reductions: The paradoxes of change and continuity in Iran and Japan. *Political Psychology 18:* 355-384.
Monroe, K.R. (Ed.). 2002. *Political Psychology*. Mahwah, NJ: Erlbaum.
Montero, M. 1986. Political psychology in Latin America. In *Political psychology: Contemporary problems and issues,* (Gen. Ed.) M.G. Hermann, pp. 414-433. San Francisco: Jossey-Bass.
Montero, M. 1986. Political Psychology in Latin America. In *Political Psychology,* (Ed.) Margaret G. Hermann. San Francisco: Jossey-Bass.
Montiel, C.J. & Chionbian, V. 1991. Political Psychology in the Philippines. *Political Psychology 12:* 759-777.
Morris, E. 2001. *Theodore Rex*. New York: Random House.
Morris, M.W. & Fu, H-Y. 2001. How does culture influence conflict resolution? A dynamic constructivist analysis. *Social Cognition 19,* 324-349.
Morris, M.W. & Peng, K. 1994. Culture and cause: American and Chinese attributions for social physical events. *Journal of Personality and Social Psychology 67:* 949-971.
Munger, M.C. 2000. Political Science and Fundamental Research. *PS: Political Science and Politics 33:* 25-30.
Mutz, D. 1999. *Impersonal Influence*. New York: Cambridge University Press.
Nesbitt-Larking, P. 2003. Complexes and cognitive complexity: Canadian contributions to political psychology. *Canadian Journal of Political Science 36:* 879-896.
Neustadt, R.E. & May, E.R. 1986. *Thinking in Time: The Uses of History for Decision Makers*. New York: Free Press.
Nisbett, R. & Cohen, D. 1996. *Culture of honor*. Boulder, CO: Westview.
Nisbett, R., Peng, K., Choi, I., & Norenzayan, A. 2001. Culture and systems of thought: Holistic versus analytic cognition. *Psychological Review 108:* 291-310.

Norenzayan, A. & Nisbett, R. 2000. Culture and causal cognition. *Current Directions in Psychological Science 9:* 132-135.
Osgood, C.E. 1962. *An alternative to war or surrender.* Urbana: University of Illinois Press.
Ottati, V.C., Tindale, R.S., Edwards, J., Bryant, F.G., Health, L., O'Connell, D.C., Suarez-Balzacar, Y. & Posavac, E.J. (Eds.). 2002. *The Social Psychology of Politics.* New York: Kluwer Academic/Plenum.
Patterson, T.E. 2002. *The vanishing voter: Public involvement in an age of uncertainty.* New York: Random House (Vintage Books).
Peng, K., & Nisbett, R. 1999. Culture, dialectics, and reasoning about contradiction. *American Psychologist 54:* 741-754.
Pennebaker, J.W., Paez, D. & Rimé, B. (Eds.) 1997. *Collective memory of political events: Social psychological perspectives.* Mahwah, NJ: Erlbaum.
Pennington, N. & Hastie, R. 1986. Evidence Evaluation in Complex Decision Making. *Journal of Personality and Social Psychology 51(2):* 242-258.
Pennington, N. & Hastie, R. 1987. Explanation Based Decision Making. *Proceedings of the 9th Annual Meeting of the Cognitive Science Society Meeting,* Volume 9: pp. 682-690. Hillsdale, N.J.: Erlbaum Associates..
Peri, Y. (Ed.) 2000. *The assassination of Yitzhak Rabin.* Stanford, CA: Stanford University Press.
Peterson, R.S. 1997. A Directive Leadership Style in Group Decision Making Can Be Both Virtue and Vice: Evidence from Elite and Experimental Groups. *Journal of Personality and Social Psychology 72(5):* 1107-1121.
Phillips, K. 2002. *Wealth and democracy: A political history of the American rich.* New York: Broadway Books.
Post, J.M. (Ed.) 2004. *Leaders and their followers in a dangerous world: The psychology of political behavior.* Ithaca: Cornell University Press.
Post, J.M. (Ed.) 2003. *The psychological assessment of political leaders: With profiles of Saddam Hussein and Bill Clinton.* Ann Arbor: University of Michigan Press.
Post, J.M. 1993. Current concepts of the narcissistic personalitiy: implications for political psychology. *Political Psychology 14:* 99-121.
Pye, L. 1961. Personal identity and political ideology. In *Political Decision Makers* Ed. Dwaine Marvick, pp. 290-313. Glencoe, IL: Free Press.
Pye, L. 1986. Political Psychology in Asia. In *Political Psychology* Ed. M.G. Hermann. San Francisco: Jossey-Bass.
Pye, L. 1997. Introduction: The elusive concept of culture and the vivid reality of personality. *Political Psychology 18:* 241-254.
Rahn, W., Sullivan, J.L. & Rudolph, T.J. 2002. Political Psychology and Political Science. In *Thinking about Political Psychology* Ed. J.H. Kuklinski. New York: Cambridge University Press.
Renshon, S.A. & J. Duckitt. (Eds.) 2000. *Political Psychology: Cultural and Crosscultural Foundations.* New York: New York University Press.
Renshon, S., & Duckitt, J. 1997. Cultural and cross-cultural political psychology: Toward the development of a new subfield. *Political Psychology 18:* 233-240.
Richmond Recorder. 1802. No. 53: July 5-7.

Robins, R.S. & Post, J.M. 1997. *Political paranoia: The psychopolitics of hatred.* New Haven: Yale University Press.
Rohter, L. 2003. Bolivia's poor proclaim abiding distrust of globalization. *The New York Times,* October 17, p. A3.
Ross, L. 1977. The intuitive psychologist and his shortcomings: Distortions in the attribution process. In *Advances in social psychology* (Vol 10) Ed. L. Berkowitz, pp. 173-220. New York: Academic Press.
Ross, M.H. 1997. The relevance of culture for the study of political psychology and ethnic conflict. *Political Psychology 18:* 299-326.
Rubenstein, R.E. 2003. The psycho-political sources of terrorism. In *The new global terrorism: Characteristics, causes, controls* Ed. C. Kegley, pp. 139-150. Upper Saddle River, NJ: Prentice Hall
Rudolph, L.I. & Rudolph, S.H. 1967. *The Modernity of Tradition: Political Development in India.* Chicago: University of Chicago Press.
Sales, S.M. 1973. Threat as a factor in authoritarianism: An analysis of archival data. *Journal of Personality and Social Psychology 28:* 44-57.
Sampson, A. 1999. *Mandela: The authorized biography.* New York: Knopf.
Sampson, E.E. 1989. The challenge of social change for psychology: Globalization and psychology's theory of the person. *American Psychologist 44:* 914-921.
Schachner, N. 1951. *Thomas Jefferson, A biography.* Vol. 1. New York: Appleton Century.
Schank, R. 1982. *Dynamic Memory: A Theory of Learning in Computers and People.* New York: Cambridge University Press.
Schank, R.C. & Abelson, R.P. 1977. *Scripts, Plans, Goals and Understanding.* Hillsdale, NJ: Lawrence Erlbaum Associates.
Schiffer, I. 1973. *Charisma: A Psychoanalytic Look at Mass Society.* Toronto: Univeristy of Toronto Press.
Schrodt, P.A. 1986. Predicting International Events using a Holland Classifier. *BYTE,* November.
Schrodt, P.A. 1991. Pattern Recognition of International Event Sequences: A Machine Learning Approach. In *Artificial Intelligence and International Politics* Ed. V.M. Hudson. Boulder: Westview Press.
Schrodt, P.A. & Gerner, D.J. 1994. Validity Assessment of a Machine Coded Event Data Set for the Middle East, 1982-1992. *American Journal of Political Science 38:* 825-854.
Schroeder-Heister, P. (Ed.) 1989. *Extensions of Logic Programming.* International Workshop, Tübingen, FRG, December.
Schwartz, S.H. 1990. Individualism-Collectivism: Critique and Proposed Refinements. *Journal of Cross-Cultural Psychology 21(2):* 139-157.
Schwartz, S. & Sagie, G. 2000. Value consensus and importance: A cross-national study. *Journal of Cross-Cultural Psychology 31:* 465-497.
Scowen, P. 2002. *Rogue nation: The America the rest of the world knows.* Toronto: McClelland & Stewart.
Sears, D.O. 2002. Long-term psychological consequences of political events. In *Political Psychology* Ed. K.R. Monroe, pp. 249-269. Mahwah NJ: Erlbaum Associates.

Sears, D.O. 1989. The Ecological Niche of Political Psychology. *Political Psychology* 10: 501-506.
Sears, D.O. 1987. Political Psychology. *Annual Review of Psychology 38*: 229-255.
Sears, D.O. & Funk, C.L. 1991. Graduate Education in Political Psychology. *Political Psychology 12:* 345-362.
Sears, D.O., Huddy, L. & Jervis, R. (Eds.). 2003. *Handbook of Political Psychology.* New York: Oxford University Press.
Senarclens, P. 1984. *Yalta.* Paris: Presses Universitaires.
Senghas, A. & Coppola, M. 2001. Children creating language: How Nicaraguan Sign Language acquired a spatial grammar. *Psychological Science 12:* 323-328.
Shamir, J., & Shikaki, K. 2002. Self-serving perceptions of terrorism among Israelis and Palestinians. *Political Psychology 23:* 537-557.
Shumao, W. 1996. Political Psychology in China. *Political Psychology 17:* 779-785.
Shweder, R. 1991. *Thinking through cultures: Expeditions in cultural psychology.* Cambridge, MA: Harvard University Press.
Silverstein, B. 1989. Enemy Images: The Psychology of U.S. Attitudes and Cognitions Regarding the Soviet Union. *American Psychologist 44(6):* 908-913.
Simon, H.A. 1985. Human Nature in Politics: The Dialogue of Psychology with Political Science. *American Political Science Review 79:* 293-305.
Simonton, D.K. 1990. *Psychology, science, and history: An introduction to historiometry.* New Haven, CT: Yale University Press.
Simonton, D.K. 2000. Creativity: Cognitive, personal, developmental, and social aspects. *American Psychologist 55:* 151-158.
Skowronek, S. 1986. Notes on the presidency in the political order. In *Studies in American Political Development* Eds. K. Orren & S. Skowronek, Vol. 1, pp. 286-302. New Haven: Yale University Press.
Skowronek, S. 1993. *The politics presidents make: Leadership from John Adams to George Bush.* Cambridge: Harvard University Press.
Smith, C.P. (Ed.) 1992. *Motivation and personality: Handbook of thematic content analysis.* Cambridge: Cambridge University Press.
Smith, C.S. 2002. For China's wealthy, all but fruited plain. *The New York Times,* May 15, p. A1.
Smith, M.B. 1968. A Map for the Analysis of Personality and Politics. *Journal of Social Issues 24*:15-28.
Smith, P. 1913. Luther's early development in the light of psycho-analysis. *American Journal of Psychology 24:* 360-377.
Sniderman, P., Brody, R., & Tetlock, P. 1991. *Reasoning and Choice: Explorations in Political Psychology.* New York: Cambridge University Press.
Snyder, R.C., Bruck, H.W., & Sapin, B. (Eds.) 1962. *Foreign Policy Decision-Making: An Approach to the Study of International Politics.* Glencoe, IL.: The Free Press.
Snyder, R.C., Bruck, H.W., & Sapin, B. (Eds.) with V.M. Hudson, D.H. Chollet, and J.M. Goldgeier. 2002. *Foreign Policy Decision Making (Revisited).* New York: Palgrave MacMillan.
Social Psychology Section: British Psychological Society (2004). Conference announcement, http://www.bps.org.uk/sub-syst/socpsy/Index.htm accessed 23 January 2004.

Sorensen, J. 2004, in press. Religion, evolution and an immunology of cultural systems. *Evolution and Cognition, 10.*
Soros, G. 2002. *George Soros on globalization.* New York: Public Affairs Press.
Speer, A. 1970. *Inside the Third Reich.* New York: Macmillan.
Staub, E. 2003. Notes on cultures of violence, cultures of caring and peace, and the fulfillment of basic human needs. *Political Psychology 24:* 1-21.
Steinberg, B.S. 1996. *Shame and Humiliation: Presidential Decision Making on Vietnam.* Pittsburgh: University of Pittsburgh press.
Steinbruner, J.D. 1974. *The cybernetic theory of decision: new dimensions of political analysis.* Princeton, N.J.: Princeton University Press.
Stone, W.F. 1976. *The Psychology of Politics.* New York: The Free Press.
Stone, W.F. 1980. The myth of left-wing authoritarianism. *Political Psychology 2:* 3-19.
Stone, W.F. (Coordinator) 2003. Psychological responses to the 2001 terrorist attacks on the United States. *Psicología Política* (Valencia, Spain), November (No. 27).
Stone, W.F. & Schaffner, P.E. 1988. *The Psychology of Politics.* New York: Springer-Verlag.
Strozier, C. 1983. *Lincoln's quest for Union: Public and private meanings.* New York: Basic Books.
Suedfeld P. 2000. Professor Boulding's Peaceable Kingdom. *Peace and Conflict: Journal of Peace Psychology 6:* 253-258.
Suedfeld, P. & Tetlock, P.E. 1977. Integrative Complexity of Communications in International Crises. *Journal of Conflict Resolution 21:* 169-184.
Suedfeld, P., Tetlock, P.E., & Ramirez, C. 1977. War, Peace and Integrative Complexity. *Journal of Conflict Resolution 21:* 427-442.
Sullivan, J.L. & Transue, J.E. 1999. The Psychological Underpinnings of Democracy: A Selective Review of Research on Political Tolerance, Interpersonal Trust, and Social Capital. *Annual Review of Psychology 50:* 625-650.
Surowiecki, J. 2002. Did Iacocca ruin American business? *The Guardian.* July 23. Retrieved November 10, 2003 from http://www.guardian.co.uk/g2/story/0,3604, 761548,00.html
Sylvan, D.A., Goel, A., & Chandrasekaran, B. 1990. Analyzing Political Decision Making from an Information Processing Perspective: JESSE. *American Journal of Political Science 34(1):* 74-123.
Sylvan, D.A., Ostrom, T. & Gannon, K. 1994 Case-Based, Model-Based, and Explanation-Based Styles of Reasoning in Foreign Policy. *International Studies Quarterly 38:* 61-90.
Sylvan, D.A. & Thorson, S.J. 1992. Ontologies, Problem Representation, and the Cuban Missile Crisis. *Journal of Conflict Resolution 36(4):* 709-732.
Sylvan, D.A. & Voss, J. (Eds.) 1998. *Problem Representation in Foreign Policy Decision Making.* New York: Cambridge University Press.
Taber, C.S. 1992. POLI: An Expert System Model of U.S. Foreign Policy Belief Systems. *American Political Science Review 86(4):* 888-904.
Taber, C.S. 1998. The Interpretation of Foreign Policy Events: A Cognitive Process Theory. In *Problem Representation in Foreign Policy Decision Making* Eds. D.A. Sylvan & J. Voss, pp. 29-52. New York: Cambridge University Press

Tanaka, A. 1984. China, China Watching, and CHINA_WATCHER. In *Foreign Policy Decision Making: Perception, Cognition, and Artificial Intelligence* Eds. D.A. Sylvan and S. Chan, pp. 310 - 344. New York: Praeger.
Tetlock, P.E. 1979. Identifying Victims of Groupthink from Public Statements of Decision-makers. *Journal of Personality and Social Psychology 37:* 1314-1324.
Tetlock, P.E. 1994. Political psychology or politicized psychology: Is the Road to Scientific Hell Paved with Good Moral Intentions? *Political Psychology 15:* 509-529.
Tetlock, P.E. 1998. Social Psychology and World Politics. In *The Handbook of Social Psychology*, Volume 2 (4th Edition) Eds. D.T. Gilbert, S.T. Fiske, & G. Lindzey, pp. 868-889. New York: McGraw Hill.
Tetlock, P.E. 1999. Theory-Driven Reasoning about Plausible Pasts and Probable Futures in World Politics: Are We Prisoners of our Preconceptions? *American Journal of Political Science 43(2):* 335-366.
Thorson, S.J. 1984. Intentional Inferencing in Foreign Policy: An AI approach. In *Foreign Policy Decision Making: Perception, Cognition, and Artificial Intelligence,* Eds. D.A. Sylvan and S. Chan, pp. 280-309. New York: Praeger
Thorson, S.J. & Sylvan, D.A. 1982. Counterfactuals and the Cuban Missile Crisis. *International Studies Quarterly 26(4):* 539-571.
Tjosvold, D. & Sun, H.F. 2003. Openness among Chinese in conflict: Effects of direct discussion and warmth on integrative decision making. *Journal of Applied Social Psychology 33:* 1878-1897.
Tocqueville, Alexis de 1874 [1836]. *De la démocratie en Amérique.*Vol. 2. Paris: Lévy.
Triandis, H.C. 1995. *Individualism and collectivism.* Boulder, CO: Westview.
Tuchman, B. W. 1962. *The guns of August.* New York: Macmillan.
Tucker, R.C. 1973. *Stalin as revolutionary, 1897-1929: A study in history and personality.* New York: Norton.
Volkan, V. 1980. Narcissistic personality organization and reparative leadership. *International Journal of Group Psychotherapy 30:* 131-152.
Volkan, V. & Itzkowitz, N. 1984. *The immortal Atatürk.* Chicago: University of Chicago Press.
Volkan, V., Itzkowitz, N., & Dod, A. 1997. *But Who Voted for Him? Richard Nixon: A Psychobiography.* New York: Columbia University Press.
Voss, J.F. 1998. On the representation of problems: An information processing approach to foreign policy decision making. In *Problem representation in foreign policy decision making.* Eds. D.A. Sylvan & J.F. Voss, pp. 8-52. Cambridge, UK: Cambridge University Press.
Waite, R.G.L. 1977. *The Psychopathic God: Adolf Hitler.* New York: Basic Books.
Walker, S.G. 1995. Psycho-dynamic Processes and Framing Effects in Foreign Policy Decision-making: Woodrow Wilson's Operational Code. *Political Psychology 16(4):* 697-717.
Walker, S.G. 1977. The Interface Between Beliefs and Behavior. *Journal of Conflict Resolution 21(1):* 129-165.
Walker, S.G. & Schafer, M. 2000. The Political Universe of Lyndon B. Johnson and His Advisors: Diagnostic and Strategic Propensities in Their Operational Codes. *Political Psychology 21(3):* 529-543.

Walker, S.G., Schafer, M. & Young, M.D. 1999. Presidential Operational Codes and Foreign Policy Conflicts in the Post-Cold War World. *Journal of Conflict Resolution 43(5):* 610-625.

Ward, D. 2002. Political Psychology: Origins and Development. In *Political Psychology* Ed. K.R. Monroe, pp. 61-78. Mahwah, NJ: Erlbaum.

Washington, G. 1983. *The papers of George Washington.* Colonial Series, Vol. 1. Charlottesville: University of Virginia Press.

Weber, M. 1968[1922]. *Economy and society: An outline of interpretive sociology.* New York: Bedminster Press.

Weber, Max 1946[1921]. Politics as a vocation. In *From Max Weber: Essays in Sociology* Eds. H. H. Gerth and C. Wright Mills, pp. 77-128. New York: Oxford University Press.

Weber, Max 1947. *The Theory of Social and Economic Organization.* (Trs.) A.M. Henderson and T. Parsons. New York: Oxford University Press.

Weber, M. 1952. *The Protestant Ethic and the spirit of capitalism.* London: Allen & Unwin.

Weiner, B. 1986. Attribution, emotion, and affect. In *Handbook of motivation and cognition: Foundations of social behavior* Eds. R. M. Sorrentino & E. T. Higgins, pp. 281-312. New York: Guilford Press.

Weiss, H. 2003. A cross-national comparison of nationalism in Austria, the Czech and Slovac Republics, Hungary, and Poland. *Political Psychology 24:* 377-401.

Welch, S., Sigelman, L., Bledsoe, T., & Combs, M. 2001. *Race and Place.* New York: Cambridge University Press.

White, R.K. (Ed.) 1986. *Psychology and the prevention of nuclear war: A book of readings.* New York: New York University Press.

Wilson, K. (Ed.) 1996. *Forging the collective memory: Government and international historians through two world wars.* Providence, RI: Berghahn Books.

Winter, D.G. 2003. The future of political psychology: New foundations and interdisciplinary methods. In *Handbook of political psychology* Eds. Kawata, J. & Araki, Y. Tokyo: Hokuju Shuppan.

Winter, D.G. 2002. An intellectual agenda for political psychology. In *Political psychology* Ed. K.R. Monroe, pp. 385-398. Mahwah, NJ: Erlbaum.

Winter, D.G. 2000. Power, sex, and violence: A psychological reconstruction of the twentieth century and an intellectual agenda for political psychology. *Political Psychology 21:* 383-404.

Winter, D.G. 1998. A Motivational Analysis of the Clinton First Term and the 1996 Presidential Campaign. *Leadership Quarterly 9(3):* 367-376.

Winter, D.G. 1987. Leader Appeal, Leader Performance, and the Motive Profiles of Leaders and Followers: A Study of American Presidents and Elections. *Journal of Personality and Social Psychology 52(1):* 196-202.

Winter, D.G. 1983. *Development of an integrated system for scoring motives in verbal running text.* Unpublished manuscript, Wesleyan University, Middletown, CT.

Winter, D.G. 1973. *The power motive.* New York: Free Press.

Winter, D.G., Hermann, M.G., Weintraub, W., & Walker, S.G. 1991a. The Personalities of Bush and Gorbachev Measured at a Distance: Procedures, Portraits, and

Policy. *Political Psychology 12(2):* 215-245.
Winter, D.G., Hermann, M.G., Weintraub, W. & Walker, S.G. 1991b. The personalities of Bush and Gorbachev at a distance: Follow-up on predictions. *Political Psychology 12:* 457-464.
Winter, D.G., Stewart, A.J., Henderson-King, E.I., & Henderson-King, D. 2001. *Moving away: Resisting the dominant culture of high school.* Paper presented at the annual meeting of the American Psychological Association, August, 2001, San Francisco.
Wituski, D.M., Clawson, R.A., Oxley, Z.M., Green, M.C. & Barr, M.K. 1998. Bridging a Disciplinary Divide: The Summer Institute in Political Psychology. *PS: Political Science and Politics 21*: 221-226.
Wolfenstein, E.V. 1967. *The Revolutionary personality: Lenin, Trotsky, Gandhi.* Princeton: Princeton University Press.
Wolfenstein, M. 1965. Death of a parent and death of a president: Children's reactions to two kinds of loss. In *Children and the Death of a President* Eds. M. Wolfenstein and G. Kliman, pp. 62-79. Garden City: Doubleday.
Yin, R.K. 1989. *Case study research: Designs and methods* (rev. Ed.). Applied social research methods series. Newbury Park, CA: Sage.
Zaller, J. 1992. *The Nature and Origins of Mass Opinion.* New York: Cambridge University Press.

About the Editor and Contributors

Linda Shepherd, Ph.D.
Editor
Associate Professor of Public Policy and Political Science
Department of Political Science
Cal Poly

Linda Shepherd is a faculty member in the department of political science, founding director of the Master of Public Policy program, and founder of the Institute for Policy Research at Cal Poly, San Luis Obispo, where she specializes in teaching interdisciplinary courses. She received her education at UCLA, the University of Washington, and the University of California, Davis. She has authored and co-authored several journal articles and book chapters on the subjects of political psychology, political behavior, public policy, and research methods. She co-edited two previous books devoted to the analysis of methods for profiling political leaders across divergent cultures and currently serves as Vice President as well as member of the Executive Board of the Psycho-Politics Research Committee within the International Political Science Association. Dr. Shepherd is the recipient of multiple research grants and has presented research at numerous national and international scholarly meetings.

Betty Glad, Ph.D.
Olin D. Johnston Professor of Political Science
Department of Political Science
University of South Carolina

Betty Glad is the Olin D. Johnston Professor of Political Science at the University of South Carolina. She has served as president of the International Society for Political Psychology, president of the Presidency Research Group of the American Political Science Association, and vice president of the American Political Science Association. In 1997 she received the Harold Lasswell Award of the International Society for Political Psychology for a lifetime of outstanding contribution to political psychology. In 2000 the American Political Science Association recognized her contributions to the field of political science in the Frank Goodnow Award. Her books include *The Russian Transformation: Political, Sociological and Psychological*

Aspects (co-editor and contributor); *Jimmy Carter: In Search of the Great White House; The Psychological Dimensions of War; Key Pittman: The Tragedy of the Senate Insider; Charles Evans Hughes and The Illusions of Innocence;* and *Striking First* (with Chris Dolan). She has appeared on several national television and radio shows including The American Experience documentary on Jimmy Carter, The McNeil Leher News Hour and National Public Radio.

Ian Hansen
University of British Columbia

Ian Hansen is a PhD Candidate at the Universtiy of British Columbia. Currently conducting research in cultural, social and political psychology, Ian received his M.A. in Psychology from the University of Illinois Urbana-Champaign and his B.A. in Philosophy from Swarthmore College. His thesis is on religion, religious intolerance and support for religious violence.

Elizabeth Marvick, Ph.D.
Professor Emeritus
University of California, Los Angeles

Elizabeth Wirth Marvick was educated at Radcliffe College (Cambridge, MA), the University of Chicago and Columbia University (PhD in Public Law and Government). During her career, she taught political and social science at the City University of New York, Claremont Graduate School, California Institute of Technology, the American University in Paris, the University of Bordeaux (as a Fulbright Lecturer in American Civilization) and the University of California, Los Angeles. Her publications included *The Young Richelieu: a Psychoanalytic Approach to Leadership* (University of Chicago Press, 1983), *Louis XIII: the Making of a King* (Yale University Press, 1986) and numerous articles applying depth psychology to the study of personality and politics. We regret to note that Dr. Marvick passed away during 2005.

Kathleen M. McGraw, Ph.D.
Professor of Political Science
Department of Political Science
The Ohio State University

Kathleen M. McGraw is Professor of Political Science at the Ohio State University. She received her PhD in Social Psychology from Northwestern University in 1985. She is a recipient of the Erik Erikson Award for Early Career Achievement from the International Society for Political Psychology, and has served as a co-director of the Summer Institute in Political Psychology at Ohio State. She has published widely in political science, political psychology, and social psychology journals.

Brent A. Strathman Ph.D.
Visiting Assistant Professor
Department of Government
Dartmouth College

Brent Strathman recently finished his dissertation, and will begin a visiting position at Dartmouth in September 2006. His research interests include international security, political psychology, leadership, and foreign policy decision-making. He is currently conducting research on existential threat and a book project based on his dissertation, tentatively titled *Winning the President's Ear: Power Politics, & Persuasin in Foreign Policy*.

Peter Suedfeld, Ph.D.
Professor of Psychology
Department of Psychology
University of British Columbia

Peter Suedfeld is Dean Emeritus of Graduate Studies and Professor Emeritus of Psychology at The University of British Columbia, Vancouver, Canada. His more than 250 publications focus on how people cope with challenging and dangerous situations. His research has used laboratory and field settings, as well as applying content analytic techniques to archived materials produced by survivors of extreme trauma (e.g., the Holocaust), leadership élites, and ordinary citizens experiencing political, ecological, economic, military, and personal crises. He has been a consultant to many agencies, including the Peace Corps, NASA, the Canadian Space Agency, and the Department of National Defence. He has served as President of the Canadian Psychological Association (CPA) and Vice President of the International Society of Political Psychology (ISPP), and on many scientific, professional, and educational committees and boards. Suedfeld is a Fellow of the Royal Society (the National Academy) of Canada, the American and Canadian Psychological Associations, the New York Academy of Sciences, and other scientific organizations. Among his honours are the Donald O. Hebb Award, the CPA's highest award for scientific contributions; the National Science Foundation's Antarctica Service Medal; the Zachor Award from the Canadian government; and the ISPP's Harold D. Lasswell Award for distinguished scientific contributions in the area of political psychology.

Donald A. Sylvan, Ph.D.
Professor of Political Science
Department of Political Science
The Ohio State University

Donald A. Sylvan (B.A. Northwestern; PhD. University of Minnesota) has been a member of the faculty of the Department of Political Science at Ohio State University since 1974. He is the author or editor of four books, including *Problem Representation in Foreign Policy Decision Making*, (Cambridge University Press, 1998), and *International Intervention: Sovereignty vs. Responsibility*, (Frank Cass, 2002); and has authored articles in journals such as *Political Psychology, International Studies Quarterly, Journal of Conflict Resolution, American Journal of Political Science,* and *Journal of Peace Research*. Current research interests include foreign policy decision making and Middle East politics. He served as President of the Foreign Policy Analysis Section of ISA, President of the Midwest Region of I.S.A, and is now Treasurer of the International Society of Political Psychology.

David G. Winter, Ph.D.
Professor of Psychology
Department of Psychology
University of Michgan

David G. Winter is Professor of Psychology at the University of Michigan. He was educated at Harvard University and the University of Oxford. He previously taught at Wesleyan University, and has been a visiting faculty member at the Massachusetts Institute of Technology, Harvard, College of the Holy Cross, University of Amsterdam, and Peking University. Winter is a personality and social psychologist with a special interest in political psychology. His research has focused on power and power motivation; the motivational bases of leadership; and the psychological aspects of conflict escalation, war, and peace. He is the author of *The Power Motive, Motivating Economic Achievement (with D. C. McClelland), A New Case for the Liberal Arts (with D. C. McClelland and A. J. Stewart)*, and *Personality: Analysis and Interpretation of Lives,* as well as numerous papers in psychological and political psychology journals. He also translated and edited Otto Rank's *The Don-Juan Legend.* He is a past president of the International Society of Political Psychology.

Index

Locators annotated with *f* indicate figures.
Locators annotated with *n* indicate footnotes.
Locators annotated with *t* indicate tables.

A

Abalakina-Paap, M.A., 82
Abelson, R.P, 93*n*
Abramson, L.Y., 117
Adair, J.G., 65, use of taxonomy for political psychology, 74-82, 76*t*, 78*t*;work of, 72-75
Adams, John, 48
Adams, H., 49
Adler, E. 95*n*, 106
Ageyev, V.S., 82
Albin, M., 120
Alexander, M., 100
Alker, H.R. Jr., 97
Alliluyeva, S., 41
Alt, J., 29
Altemeyer, B., use of right-wing authoritarianism scale, 82; American Political Science Association, 26, 26*n*; political psychology section, 26, 126; awards, 26
Amin, Idi: Uganda and, 45
Applied Psychology: International Congress of, 126
Araki, Y., 30
Ardila, R., 20*n*, 69
Arian, A., 31
Arnett, J.J., 113

B

Banerjee, S., 95-96
Barbaranelli, C., 56
Barber, B.R., 120
Barber, J.D.: study of presidential character, 47, 57-58
Barner-Barry, C., 30
Barr, M.K., 27
Barringer, F., 115*n*
Bar-Tal, D., 19, 28
Benet-Martinez, V., 84
Berger, M.: on personality of leaders in democratic systems, 42
Bersoff, D.M., 83
Bickerton, D., 83
bin Laden, Osama, 120
Blanchard, W., 44
Bledsoe, T., 31
Bloom, R., 32
Bolshevik personality studies, 37
Boulding, E., 85
Boulding, K., 100
Boyer, P., 83
Brady, H.E., 61
Brenner, C., 43
Breslauer, G., 59, 60
Brewer, M., 27, 100
Brody, R., 20, 31
Bromberg, N., 41
Brown, D., 70
Brown, R.W., 116
Bruck, H.W., 88, 89, 90, 106, 107, 108
Bryder, T., 20*n*, 111*n*
Brzezinski, Zbigniew, 54
Bullitt, W.C., 53
Burke, J.P., 61
Burns, J.M., 44
Burrows, E.G., 44
Bush, George W., 116
Byram, M., 97*n*, 107, 108

161

C
Campbell, J.D., 83
Caprara, G.V., 56
Carbonell, J.G., 93n
Carroll, J.D., 93n
Carter, Jimmy: advisers and, 53-54; Iranian hostage crisis and, 56
Cederman, L., 107
Chandrasekaran, B., 91, 92, 106, 107
Chang, H-C., 82
Chiongbian, V.M., 20n, 69
Chirot, D., 64, 70
Chiu, C-Y., 82, 83
Choi, I., 83
Chollet, D.H., 108
Chong, D., 31
Christie, D.J., 61
Chua, A., 117, 118n
Churchill, Winston, 40
Clark, L.C., 36
Clawson, R.A., 27
Clemetson, L., 116
Clinton, Bill: Public reaction to sexual scandal, 55
Cohen, D., 84
Cold War, 110, 111
Combs, M., 31; complexity conceptual/integrative, 104-105
Converse, J., 110
Coppola, M., 83
Cottam, R., 89, 100
Christensen, C., 97
Crosby, F., 117
Crystal, D.S., 85
Cultural psychology: political psychology and, 81-86

D
Dallek, R., 52
Davies, J.C., 117
Dávila, J.M., 63
De Gaulle, Charles, 46; narcissism and, 46; Roosevelt and, 52
De Grazia, S., 36, 55
de Klerk: and Nelson Mandela, 44, 51

De Landtsheer, C., 70
Delli Carpini, M.X., 31
DeNardo, J., 31
Deutsch, M., 33
Devlin, R.J., 120
Dias, M.G., 84
Dille, B., 105
DiRenzo, G.J., 30
Dod, A., 46
Domhoff, G.W., 117
Dorna, A., 69
Doty, R.M., 116
Driver, M.J., 105
Duckitt, J., 30, 86, 130
Duffy, G., 93, 97

E
Educational Testing Service: salary bonuses and, 116
Ego: identity, 38-39; mechanisms of defense, 38-39
Eisenhower, D.D., 47; family experiences, 47-48; Hungarian uprising and, 57; Korea and, 60; McCarthy, dealings with, 49; personality, 48; Vietnam and, 60-61; Washington, compared to, 49-50; World War II decisions, 48
(EISPP) European Summer Institute in Political Psychology, 28, 68
Elms, A.C., 30
Erikson, E.H., 39, 44, 120
Erikson, R., 31
Estes, T., 48; on George Washington, 48-49, 49-50

F
Face: as concept, 82
Fairbank, J.K., 125
Feldman, O., 20n, 65, 69-70, 80
Feldman, S., 26, 29
Fenichel, O., 41
Fischerkeller, M., 100
Fisher, I., 116
Fiske, A.P., 86

Fiske, D.W., 114
Fleming, 97*n*, 107, 108
Flügel, J.C., 36
foreign policy decision making: at-a-distance approaches and, 103-105; computational approaches to, 89-90; belief models, 93-94, 97; hermeneutic models, 95-96, 97; scripts and, 91*n*; rule-based, 90-93, 97; experimental approaches and, 95-101; cognitive processes and, 100-101; cognitive structures and, 99-100; linguistics and, 97; pattern-matching and, 102-103
Founding Fathers: similarity of upbringing, 51
Freedman, A.E., 30
Freedman, P.E., 30
Freud, A., 39
Freud, S., 36, 53
Friedman, T.L., 120
Fu, H-Y., 85, 86
Funk, C.L., 24

G
Gannon, K., 91, 100-101
Garzón, A., 87
George, A., 36-37, 38, 53, 103, 130
George, J., 36-37, 38, 53
Gerner, D.J., 102
Gandhi, Mohandas, 120; transformation of narcissistic process and, 44
Gibson, J., 31
Giles, M.W., 21
Gilpin, R., 112
Glad, B. 42, 43-44, 46-47, 50, 51, 53-54, 55, 56, 57, 58, 60, 131-132; on tyrants, 47
globalization, 111-115; agenda of political psychology and, 121-127; aggression and, 121;attractions and preconditions of, 113-114; charismatic leaders and, 120-121; dangers and risks of, 114; income inequality and, 116-118, 121; individualism and, 114-115; protests to and globalizers' response, 121; skepticism and malaise associated with, 118-120; threat and paranoia associated with, 115-116
Goel, A., 92, 106, 107
Goldgeier, J.M., 108
Goldhamer, H., 53, 54
Goldwater machine, 93*n*
Gorbachev, Mikhail: reform and, 44, 50, 59-60
Gorer, G., 37
Gouws, A., 31
Graber, D., 18*n*
Green, M.C., 27
Greenberg, W.J., 97
Greenstein, F.I., 21, 29, 47, 55, 61; on Eisenhower, 47
Groupthink, *see* Janis
Gulf War, 119

H
Haidt, J., 84
Hankey, Maurice, 54
Hardt, M., 112
Hartmann, H., 39
Harvey, J. H., 117
Hastie, R., 90-91, 97, 98, 100-101
Heeger, G., 120
Heine, S.J., 83
Heitmeyer, W., 118
Held, J., 69
Henderson-King, D., 114
Henderson-King, E.I., 114
Hermann, M.G., 19, 26, 27, 29, 33, 69, 73, 100, 104, 105, 129, 131
Herrmann, R.K., 27, 100, 101, 139
Hibbing, J., 31
Hitler, Adolph, 110, 120, 130 malignant narcissism and, 41-42; identification with Martin Luther, 40-41
Ho, D.Y.F., 82
Holsti, O.R., 56, 101
Holt, R.G., 82

163

Hong, Y., 84, 85
Hopf, T., 95*n*, 106, 108
Huckfeldt, R., 31
Huddy, L., 26, 29, 30, 31
Hudson, V.M., 90, 96, 106
Hume, David, 125
Hunt, L., 43
Hunt, W.B., 70
Huntington, S.P., 85
Hurwitz, R., 97

I
Iacocca, L.A., 115
Individualism: globalization and, 114-115
International Political Science Association, 26
International Society of Political Psychology (ISPP), 126; annual book series, 26; awards, 26; conferences and, 26; international, 67-68*t*; future plans and, 34; handbook and, 26; homepage for, 26; international collaborations and, 72*t*; Internet and, 31-32; journal and, 25-26; ranking and, 25-26; newsletter and, 26, 27, 31-32; membership and, 25; international membership and, 25, 65-66, 66*t*; regional membership and, 66*t*; overview of, 25-27
International Studies Association, 26-27
Itzkowitz, N., 44, 46
Iyengar, S., 18*n*, 29, 111

J
Janis, I.L., 56, 71, 101
Janofsky, M., 115
Jefferson, Thomas, 41; personality, 48
Jervis, R., 19, 20, 23, 26, 30, 71, 89, 103, 132
Jihad, 120
Job, B.L, 91-92, 106
Johnson, D., 91-92, 106
Johnson, Lyndon: hostility to, 55; Vietnam and, 60-61
Johnson, P.J., 87
Joll, J., 124
Jones, E., 36, 43
Jutras, H.: the novel *Quebec is Killing Me* and, 113

K
Kaczynski, T.: unabomber manifesto and, 118-119
Kahn, J., 116
Kahneman, D., 108
Kaplan, R.D., 112
Katz, I.M., 83
Kauffman, S., 103
Kawata, J., 30
Kearns Goodwin, D., 57, 61
Kecskemeti, P., 37
Kemal, Mustafa, 44, 45-46; family experiences, 45; Turkish revolution and, 44
Kennedy, John F.: assassination of, 55; Cuban missile crisis and, 57-58, 91-92, 124, 130; Khrushchev and, 57, 130
Kennedy, P.M., 125
Khong, Y.F., 70, 101
Kilborn, P.T., 116
Kille, K.J., 71
Kimmel, P., 86
Kinder, D.R., 18*n*
King, Martin Luther, Jr., 120
Kinnvall, C., 33
Kitayama, S., 83
Kitts, K., 57
Kissinger, H. 103
Klandermans, B., 71
Klein, J.T., 110, 126
Knollenberg, B., 46
Knutson, J., 25, 29-30
Kohut, H.: influence on psychobiographies, 40-41; theory of, 40-41
Kohut, T., 51; on charismatic leaders, 55
Koller, S.H., 84

Kolodner, J.L., 100
Kossowska, M., 71
Kressel, N.J., 30
Krosnick, J.A., 18, 27
Khrushchev, Nikita, 57-58, 130
Kuklinski, J.H., 30, 31

L
Lamare, J.W., 20*n*, 69
Lane, R.E., 55, 133
Langer, W.C., 41
Laslett, P., 112
Lasswell, H.D., 36-38, 39-40, 55, 71, 110, 130, 133 Lau, R.R., 30*n*
Lavallee, L.F., 83
Le Bon, G., 63
Leaders: adaptation to environment, 58-61; advisers and, 53-54; charisma and, 54-55; development of democratic, 39; differential adaptation to crises, 56-58; followers and, 54-56; narcissism and, 39-40; problems conducting research on, 56; regime characteristics and, 42-47; style and, 47-50
Lebow, R.N., 58
left-wing authoritarianism, 82; myth of, 82
Lehman, D.R., 71, 82, 83
Leites, N., 36-37, 38, 46, 103
Lerner, M., 29, 55
Lewin, K., 19-20
Lewis, B., 117*n*, 119-120
Levi, A., 105
Levin, S., 24
Lincoln, Abraham: narcissism of, 40
Link, M., 53
Lodge, Henry Cabot, 37
Lodge, M., 30*n*
Louis XIII: influence of Cardinal Richelieu, 38; personality, 38
Long, S., 31
Loewenheim, F.L., 52
Luther, Martin, 36, 40

Lupia, A., 31, 32, 33, 35
Lynn, K., 44

M
Macdonald, S., 70
Mackenzie, W.J.M., 42
Mackuen, M., 31
Maddi, S.R., 114
Mallery, J.C., 97
Mandela, N., 44-45, 120; and de Klerk, 44, 51; family experiences, 45-46
Marcus, G., 31, 133
Marfleet, B. G., 103
Markus, H.R., 83
Marvick, E., 38, 41, 45, 49, 51, 53, 132
Marxism, 111*n*
Masuda, T., 83
May, E.R., 101
McClelland, D.C., 114, 122, 125
McCubbins, M.D., 31, 35
McDermott, R., 132
McFarland, S., 82
McGraw, K.M., 18, 27, 30*n*, 33, 131
McGuire, W.J., 20, 29, 111
McVeigh, Timothy: Oklahoma City bombing and, 119
Meeus, W.H.J., 86
Meredith, M., 45
Michener, J.A.: his novel *Poland*, 113
Micklethwait, J., 112
Milburn, T.W., 20*n*, 61, 69
Miller, J., 70
Miller, J.G., 83
Mintz, A., 29
Mishal, S., 71, 86
Mizell, F., 21
models, *see* foreign policy decision making
Moghaddam, F.M., 85
Mondale, Walter, 54
Monroe, K.R., 18, 30, 131
Montero, M., 20*n*, 111*n*
Montiel, C.J., 20*n*, 69
Morag, N., 71, 86
Morris, M.W., 84, 85, 86

motivation, 104
Mutz, D., 31, 32

N
Nazi personality studies, 37
Negri, A., 112
Nelson, T., 27
Nesbitt-Larking, P., 69
Neustadt, R.E., 101
Nisbett, R., 83, 84, 85
Nixon, Richard, 46
(NSF) National Science Foundation, 32-33
Narcissism: personality and, 43-44; psychobiographies and, 40
Norenzayan, A., 83

O
The Ohio State University, 18n; Mershon Center, 27; Summer Institute in Political Psychology, *see* SIPP
operational codes, 103-104
Osgood, C.E., 71
Ostrom, T., 91, 100-101
Ottati, V.C., 30
Oxley, Z.M., 27

P
Paez, D., 70
Patterson, D., 21
Patterson, T.E., 118, 118n
Peng, K., 83, 84, 85
Pennebaker, J.W., 70
Pennington, N., 91, 100, 101
Peri, Y., 69
Peterson, B.E., 116
Peterson, R.S., 101
Phillips, K., 116
Piagetian development theory: use of, *See* Banerjee
Plato, 132
Political psychology: cultural psychology and, 81-86; definition, 18-19; as related to international issues, 63-65; formal degree programs, 23-25; globalization and, *see* globalization; historical perspective and, 124-125; humanities and, 125; individualized courses of study, 23-24; international journals, 65, 68; international organizations, 67-68; internationalization of, 72-81, 76t, 78t; Internet and, 31-32; journal references, 21-24, 21n, 22t; methodological pluralism and, 125-127; perspective in, 19-20, 130-131; political economy and, 22-23; political science contribution to, 123; professional associations, 25-27; psychology contribution to, 122; rational choice and, 32-33, 35, 131-133; research funding and, 32-34; research, international, 69-71; resources, 25-27; scholarly journals and, 22t, 22-23; seminars in, 28-29; spiral analysis and, 37-38; summer institutes, *see* SIPP and ESIPP; theoretical diversity and, 70-71; undergraduate education and, 24-25, 34; volumes on international focus, 69-70; overview of, 29-31; workshops in, 28-29
Pool, I., 36
Popkin, S.L., 32
Post, J., 40, 42, 43, 44, 73, 130
Power, 111; narcissism and, 39-40
Prospect theory, 132
Psycho-politics research committee (RC 29), *see* International Political Science Association
Puhan, B.N., 72
Pye, L., 20n, 39, 86, 111n

R
Raaijmakers, Q.A.W., 86
Rahn, W., 21n, 27
rational choice, 21n, 33
Ramirez, C., 105

Rawls, J., 133
Reagan, Ronald, 46
Renshon, S., 30, 86, 130
Reykowski, J., 28, 87
Rickman, J., 37
Rimé, B., 70
Robins, K., 42
Robins, R.S., 42
Rohter, L., 116
Roman Empire, 113, 124-125
Roosevelt, F.D.: Churchill and, 52; De Gaulle and, 52; Great Depression and, 57; response to his death, 55; Stalin and, 52
Rosenwein, R., 30
Ross, M.H., 86
Rubenstein, R.E., 120, 130
Rudolph, L., 39, 44
Rudolph, S., 39, 44
Rudolph, T.J., 21n
Rwanda: research on, 74

S
Sagie, G., 86
Sales, S.M., 116
Sampson, A., 45
Sampson, E.E., 122
Sapin, B., 88, 89, 90, 106, 107, 108
Schachner, N., 49
Schafer, M., 103
Schaffner, P.E., 30
Schaller, M., 82
Schank, R.C, 93n, 100
Schiffer, I., 55
Schrodt, P.A., 102
Schroeder-Heister, P., 97n, 107
Schwartz, S., 86
Schwartz, S.H., 70
Scowen, P., 124
Scully, R.M., 71
Sears, D.O., 19, 20, 23, 24-25, 26, 30n, 30, 55
Seligman, M.E.P., 64, 70, 117
Senarclens, P., 53
Senghas, A., 83

Shakespeare, William, 126
Shamir, J., 71
Shapiro, R., 29, 31
Shikaki, K., 71
Shiraev, E., 60
Shumao, W., 20n
Shweder, R., 82
Sigelman, L., 31
Silverstein, B., 100
Simon, A.F., 18n, 132
Simon, H.A., 90
Simonton, D.K., 122, 126
(SIPP) The Summer Institute in Political Psychology, 18n, 27-28
Skowronek, S., 60
Slovic, P., 108
Small, V.V., 41
Smith, C.P., 86
Smith, C.S, 116
Smith, M.B., 20
Smith, P., 36
Sniderman, P., 20, 31
Snyder, R.C., 88, 89-90, 106, 107, 108
Social constructivism: political psychology and, 106
Social Sciences and Humanities Research Council of Canada, 87
Sorensen, J., 85
Soros, G., 112
Speer, A., 40, 41
Sprague, J., 31
St. Paul, 113, 113n
Stalin, 110, 130; malignant narcissism and, 41
Staub, E., 74, 85
Steinberg, B., 42, 46, 60
Steinbruner, J.D., 89
Stewart, A.J., 114
Stimson, J., 31
Stone, W.F., 30, 71, 82
Strozier, C., 40
Suedfeld, P., 85, 104-105
Sullivan, J.L. 18n, 21n, 31
Sun, H.F., 70
Surowiecki, J., 115, 117n

167

Svetik, I., 87
Sylvan, D.A., 90-91, 92, 100, 101, 106, 107, 108

T
Taber, C.S., 26, 94, 98, 107
Tanaka, A., 97, 98
Teasdale, J.D., 117
ter Bogt, T.F.M., 86
Terrorism: charismatic leaders and, 120; September 11th groupthink and, 56-57
Tetlock, P., 18n, 20, 27, 31, 34, 86, 101, 104, 105
Theiss-Morse, E., 31
Thorson, S.J., 91, 92, 108
Tibet: culture and liberation of, 85
Tjosvold, D., 70
Tocqueville, A. de: opinion of American leaders, 42
Transue, J.E., 18n
Trapnell, P.D., 83
Triandis, H.C., 70
Tuchman, B.W.: *The Guns of August* and, 124
Tucker, R.C., 41
Tucker, S.A., 93
Tversky, A., 108

U
Unabomber manifesto, *See* Kaczynski
University of Michigan: President's salary and, 116

V
Valenty, L., 70
Van Hiel, A., 71
Visser, P., 20, 101
Vohra, N., 72
Volkan, V., 39-40, 44, 46
Voss, J., 92, 108

W
Waite, R.G.L., 41
Walker, S.G., 103, 104

Wallace, M., 44
Ward, D., 24, 29, 30, 66t
Washington, George, 44, 45; Eisenhower, compared to, 49-50; family experiences, 45; in French and Indian War, 41; paranoia and, 46; presidency, 48-50
Weary, G., 117
Weber, M., 39, 54-55, 62, 84, 115, 115n
Weiner, B., 117
Weintraub, W., 104
Weiss, H., 71
Weiszbeck, T., 87
Welch, S., 31
White, R.K., 110
Wilson, K., 124
Wilson, Woodrow, 103; childhood experiences, 38; Colonel House and, 53-54; Henry Cabot Lodge and, 37; League of Nations and, 37; personality, 37
Winter, D.G., 104, 105, 111, 114, 114n, 116, 129, 133
Wituski, D.M., 27
Wolfenstein, E.V., 44; on study of father-son relationships and tyrants, 43; on death of Kennedy, 55
Wood, S., 31
Wooldridge, A., 112
World Trade Organization: 1999 Seattle meeting and, 114-115
World War I, 123; teachings of Nietzsche and, 124
World War II, 13, 36, 48, 52, 101; survey techniques and, 110-111

Y
Yeltsin, Boris: and childhood experience, 51; reform and, 50-51, 59
Young, M.D., 103, 105

Z
Zaller, J., 31
Zimbardo, P.G., 5